The Burden of Being Civilized

The Burden of Being Civilized

An Anthropological Perspective on the Discontents of Civilization

MILES RICHARDSON AND MALCOLM C. WEBB, EDITORS

Southern Anthropological Society Proceedings, No. 18
Mary W. Helms, Series Editor

The University of Georgia Press
Athens and London

Published by the University of Georgia Press
Athens, Georgia 30602

Set in 11 on 13 Times Roman
The paper in this book meets the guidelines for
permanence and durability of the Committee on
Production Guidelines for Book Longevity of the
Council on Library Resources.

Printed in the United States of America

90 89 88 87 86 5 4 3 2 1

Library of Congress Cataloging in Publication Data

Main entry under title:
The burden of being civilized.
(Southern Anthropological Society proceedings; no. 18)
Includes papers presented at a symposium, held in Baton Rouge, Feb. 12–14, 1983, as part of the annual meeting of the Southern Anthropological Society.
Bibliography: p.
Includes index.
1. Civilization—Congresses. 2. Social evolution—Congresses. I. Richardson, Miles, 1932– . II. Webb, Malcolm C. III. Southern Anthropological Society. IV. Series.
GN2.S9243 no. 18 [HM101] 301 s [909] 85-14072
ISBN 0-8203-0818-8 (alk. paper)
ISBN 0-8203-0832-3 (pbk.: alk. paper)

To our teachers,

William G. Haag and Leslie A. White

Contents

Preface

Civilization, once considered the pinnacle in art, science, and virtue, seems now—after Vietnam, after Watergate, after Three Mile Island, after Love Canal—almost cancerous, a self-induced malignancy that threatens to blacken the human spirit. To examine the state of civilization and to ascertain its cost are the purposes of this collection of anthropological essays.

Anthropology is uniquely qualified for such a task. Born from a union between civilization and primitive culture, it has developed into a comprehensive science of humankind. That total perspective is well represented in the present volume. Contributions from physical anthropology and archaeology join with those from linguistics and ethnology to review civilization's record in the prehistoric South, in Anglo-America, in Hispanic America, in Europe, and in Africa. The points raised by the factual essays are broadened by the theoretical ones, and together the two sorts form a provocative, exciting volume.

In preparing these proceedings of the Southern Anthropological Society, the editors have received assistance from many people, and we are honored to recognize them. We thank the participants in the key symposium, "Civilization and Its Discontents," held in Baton Rouge, February 12–14, 1983, as part of the annual meeting of the Southern Anthropological Society. A portion of the papers given during the symposium became the essays in this volume, but all of the papers that were presented enhanced our understanding of the topic. For their support of the SAS meeting we are grateful to Dr. Henry L. Snyder, Dean of the College of Arts and Sciences, and Dr. Milton B. Newton, Chairman of the Department of Geography and Anthropology, at Louisiana State University. We also thank the graduate students in the Department of Geography and Anthropology for their most generous and valuable aid. We want to recognize especially the contribution of Dr.

Anna Nardo, Department of English, LSU, for her part in making the meeting, which was held in conjunction with the Anthropological Association for the Study of Play and the American Ethnological Society, such a success. We are grateful to Dr. Jill Brody both for her work at the meeting and for her advice on editorial matters. We are appreciative of Maria Cashion and Maudrie Monceaux for their help with the manuscripts. Finally, we are saddened by the most untimely death of Dr. Marshall Durbin, but we are thankful that we have the opportunity to publish his thoughtful essay.

Miles Richardson
Malcolm C. Webb

The Burden of Being Civilized

The Concept of Civilization in Anthropology: A Critical Review

Hans A. Baer

Anthropologists have defined and regarded "civilization" in a wide variety of (often diametrically opposing) ways. Whereas most eighteenth- and nineteenth-century social philosophers, as well as some twentieth-century anthropologists, have viewed civilization as a higher moral order, other anthropologists, following in the critical tradition of Rousseau, Marx, Engels, and Morgan, have argued that it is the root of our basic discontents. In reviewing the theoretical and ideological implications of these various concepts of civilization, I will argue that a critical interpretation is essential if anthropology is to become a meaningful aid to humanity in transcending the apparently inevitable but, we must hope, reversible outcome of the civilization process: namely, the development of social stratification.

PROSPECTIVE AND RETROSPECTIVE VIEWS OF CIVILIZATION

As Wessman (1981, 33) observes, civilization is "an ill-defined concept with an interesting history." Following Stanley Diamond (1964; 1974), anthropological interpretations of civilization can be termed "prospective" or "retrospective." Both views have their roots in the Enlightenment of the eighteenth century. The prospective position, which was adopted by Condorcet and most of the nineteenth-century evolutionists, including Tylor, Frazier, Maine, and Spencer, assumes that progress is synonymous with technological and social structural complexity, culminating, of course, in modern civilization or industrial capitalism. In contrast, the retrospective position, which was first exemplified in the works of Rousseau, then Marx, and still later (to some extent) Morgan, regards progress as advancement to a better human condition—not simply evolution, social transformation, or capital accumulation. Diamond carefully makes a distinction between the retrospective position and primitivism. In contrast to the latter, which in essence is a nostalgic or romantic desire to return to the past, authentic progress involves a dialectic between past and present. "Rousseau, alienated by the rising bourgeoisie, the new urbanism, the pervading commercialism and acquisitiveness, the droning bureaucracies and the estrangement of men from natural and human rhythms, devoted most of his energies to the retrospective search for the means of uniting technical education and a more fully human socialization; and he addressed himself to the role of human volition in the formation and acceptance of government" (Diamond 1974, 219). In actuality, most modern anthropologists do not consistently adopt one or the other of these positions but, rather, ambivalently combine them.

Whereas the term "civilization" was and continues to be associated in the popular mind with purportedly higher forms of moral, aesthetic, and social cultivation, early anthropologists often used the term synonymously with the term "culture." This is most obvious in the opening sentence of *Primitive Culture* (1920), where Tylor tells us that "Culture or Civilization, taken in its wide ethnographic sense, is that complex whole which includes knowledge, belief, art, morals, law, custom, and any other capabilities and habits acquired by man as a member of society." Conversely, although Tylor frequently interchanges the terms in his book, he also differentiates the two, particularly in employing the classical evolutionary scheme (the three stages of savagery, barbarism, and civilization).

In keeping with both the prospective position and Tylor's diagnostic approach, many anthropologists have defined civilization as an assemblage of cultural traits, complexes, and institutions. Morgan (1964, 18) notes that civilization began "with the use of a phonetic alphabet and the production of literary records." He also made a lasting contribution to anthropological theory, however, by distinguishing between "primitive society" (*societas*) based upon kinship ties and "civil society" (*civitas*) organized upon the basis of property relations and territory. Childe (1950) associated civilization with urban life and delineated ten criteria from the archaeological record to distinguish the earliest cities. Currently, Sanders and Price follow the diagnostic approach in their definition of civilizations as "large social systems characterized by intense social stratification and economic specialization." They suggest that "monumental architecture is perhaps the best index of the degree of complexity of social systems" (Sanders and Price 1968, 74, 140).

According to Marvin Harris (1968, 192), "the terms 'primitive' and 'civilized' were regarded as offensive to the principle of cultural relativism" during the Boasian period. While this may have been true of many of Boas's students, it was not true of Boas himself, as indicated by his title *The Mind of Primitive Man* (1938), and his contrast between "modern civilization" and "primitive culture" in *Anthropology and Modern Life* (1928). Despite his staunch defense of the integrity of primitive cultures and his doubt about cultural development as a road to ethical betterment, Boas also expressed a prospective orientation. He argued, for example, that the advancement of civilization results in an overall increase in logical thinking and a broadening of fellowship, the latter exemplified in nationalism.

Boas's most distinguished student, Alfred Kroeber, devoted the latter part of his career to the study of the civilizational process. Although Kroeber (1963, 10–17) also attempted to define civilization in terms of certain diagnostic features—such as the existence of multiple languages or a lingua franca; elaborate political, military, and religious institutions; and economic surplus—he regarded "style" as probably the best indicator of civilizational status. "A civilization, as the assemblage of the styles followed by the inhabitants of a certain area through a certain duration of time, would thus consist of a style or manner of government, added to a style of law, and another of social relations; further, a characteristic manner of production and economy, of religious belief and organization; plus what we ordinarily call its styles of literature, art, music, and building" (Kroeber 1963, 40). A style—defined as a coherent and integrated pattern of performing things—forms, develops, matures, and dissolves or disintegrates over time. Although style constitutes the most sensitive barometer of cultural change, Kroeber argued that the causes of styles are difficult, if not impossible, to determine; at best, all that can be done is to describe the circumstances under which they form.

Despite his rejection of emotional or a priori assumptions about the superiority of civilization, Kroeber was much more of a prospectivist than his mentor, regarding primitive cultures as "infantile both in their unabashed preoccupation with bodily functions and disregard of human lives," as opposed to civilized cultures, which seem to be "psychologically more adult." He maintained that the progressive nature of civilization could be objectively demonstrated by "the quantitative expansion of the content of total human culture; the atrophy of magic based on psychopathology; the decline of infantile obsession with the outstanding physiological events of human life; and the persistent tendency of technology and science to grow accumulatively" (Kroeber 1948, 301, 304).

Extensive use of the terms "primitive" and "civilized" were reintroduced in anthropology first with Redfield's (1947) folk-urban continuum and White's (1949; 1959) efforts to revive cultural evolutionism. Toward the end of his life, Redfield (1962, 370) admitted that the "urban" end of his classic continuum might be more appropriately called "civilized." Obviously combining British structural functionalism and American historical particularism, Redfield viewed civilization as simultaneously a "societal structure" and a "historical" or "cultural structure." On the one hand, he defined civilization as "a system, or typical persisting arrangement of parts, in which the parts are kinds of people in characteristic relationships with one another"; on the other hand, he maintained that "a civilization may be thought of, then, as a structure of tradition, that is, as a persisting form of arrangements for the handing down of cultural substance (idea and its products), within a great community, the community of that civilization, and as the characteristic process for transmitting it" (Redfield 1962, 375, 392–93). In the latter approach, civilization has two interrelated components: the "great tradition of the reflective few" and the "little tradition of the largely unreflective many" (Redfield 1956).

Contrary to Diamond's (1974, 222) assertion that Redfield was a "brilliant retrospectivist at heart," it seems that Redfield clearly became a prospectivist in the last years of his life, regarding civilization as the antithesis of "folk" or primitive society. Primitive society emphasizes the "moral order," which is based on human sentiments as to what is right, over the "technical order," in which social relationships are based upon expediency and sometimes coercion (Redfield 1953). The moral order and internal cohesion of primitive society are disrupted by the technological and commercial changes that accompany the development of civilization. While the moral order predominates over the technical order in primitive society, Redfield maintained that in civilization the technical order—although greatly expanded—does not necessarily take precedence over the moral order. Instead, the moral takes on a new greatness in civilization and is accompanied by new visions, ideas, religious teachings, and ethical standards. Redfield (1953, 163) believed that with the rise of civilization, "on the whole the human race has come to develop a more decent and humane measure of goodness—there has been a transformation of ethical judgment which makes us look at uncivilized peoples, not as equals, but as people on a different level of human experience."

In his list of prospectivists, Diamond includes Leslie White, since he mechanically associated cultural evolution or progress with the amount of energy harnessed per capita per year. Conversely, Diamond (1974, 223) admits that White "has managed to refrain from an enthusiastic assessment of the present condition of civilization, and has written emphatically of primitive world view, even if in the vein of a *post mortem,* in the ethnological custom." White's view of civilization or "civil society" was strongly shaped by Morgan's distinction between *societas* and *civitas.* Because the zenith of his career coincided closely with the Cold War era, he chose not to make explicit his intellectual debt to Marx and Engels, both of whom were also impressed by Morgan's work (Carneiro 1981a). Nevertheless, in contrast to the configurational or integrative conceptions of civilization presented by Kroeber and Redfield, White recognized its exploitative and conflictual dimensions.

Despite his naive acceptance of the benefits of nuclear energy, reiterated in Ribeiro's (1968) discussion of the "civilizational process," I believe that White was more of a retrospectivist than Diamond concedes. White's assessment of primitive societies was always positive; he asserted that because they placed human relationships above property relations, they are humane, ethical, and personal systems that focus on meeting human needs. His assessment of civilization was much more severe:

> The economic systems of civil society . . . subordinating as they do human rights and human welfare to property rights, are impersonal, nonhuman, and nonethical in character. These traits translated into terms of human experience are impersonal, inhuman, inhumane, and unethical.

> All the suffering, indignities, and degradation that come from slavery, serfdom, prostitution, usury, dependence upon wages, unemployment, wars of conquest and expropriation, colonial rule, and exploitation are inherent in the economic systems of civil society. In commercial systems, anything may be bought or sold: a woman's chastity, a judge's honor, a citizen's allegiance. There is no crime however heinous that men will not commit in obedience to their economic systems. And the unethical nature of civil society's economic systems corrupts and blights the higher classes as well as the lower. (White 1959, 330)

White later modified his optimism—one shared by most conservatives, liberals, and radicals—about the capacity of technology to provide a more secure life for humanity: "Cultural systems are moving rapidly to make the earth uninhabitable. And over all hovers the specter of annihilation by two lethal cultural devices: nuclear bombs and national sovereignty" (White 1975, 11).

Following in the retrospective tradition, particularly of Marx and Engels, Lawrence Krader (1976, 6) characterized civil society as a "class-divided, class-opposed society." In his definition of civil society as the "organization of society" or the "society of political economy," he makes a concerted effort to distinguish it from the state. Although the two have been defined synonymously in the past, Krader (1976, 22) considers the state to be "the organization of society of the control and regulation of the relations within and between the classes of society; the society in question being civil society." Civil society as the organization of production in society exists in a rudimentary form in the Asiatic mode of production, takes on a more elaborate form under the ancient and feudal modes, and becomes concretely expressed in modern capitalism.

Stanley Diamond himself is the leading proponent of the retrospective view in anthropology today. Like Morgan, Redfield, White, and others, he attempts to comprehend civilization by contrasting it with primitive society. Primitive societies, with their strong sense of egalitarianism, democracy, personalism, individuation, nurturance, and the ritual celebration of life, illuminate "the dark side of a world civilization which is in chronic crisis" (Diamond 1974, 160). He argues that civilized peoples create the concept of the primitive as a response to their alienation and their desperate search for human identity. While he probably simplifies reality by explaining the rise of civilizations as a consequence "not of some environmental or technical imperative, but of the new possibilities of power which men in certain positions found it necessary to cultivate and legitimate" (Diamond 1974, 17), his contention that the benefits of civilization accrue to the few at the expense of the many seems difficult to deny. Despite the fact that peasants and workers may act as unwitting accomplices to their own exploitation—often as a result of the hegemonic influences of religion, education, and the mass media—in the end, civilization has always been imposed and necessitates continual conquest and repression.

Although primitive peoples have often been curious about civilization and have chosen to incorporate some of its dimensions into their own cultures, they have never elected to civilize themselves. Rather, civilization has always expanded hand in hand with imperialism, colonialism, neocolonialism, institutional religion, economic exploitation, and social stratification. Civilizations are themselves in continual conflict both internally and externally. In the last several centuries modern civilization has incorporated ancient civilizations and, in addition to using primitive and peasant peoples for the building of stratified nation-states, has transformed some of them into subproletariats and an increasing number of others into superfluous beings (as is exhibited by the high unemployment rates in Third World countries) whose lives are spent in continual idleness, hunger, rootlessness, and deprivation.

LOOKING BEYOND CIVILIZATION

Compared with primitive societies and even archaic civilizations, industrial civilization is a recent phenomenon. In its present form, as Bodley (1976, 3) observes, "industrialization has become a global process that has destroyed or transformed all previous cultural adaptations and has given man the power not only to bring about his own extinction as a species, but also to speed the extinction of many other species and to alter basic biological and geological processes as well." In essence, modern civilization has produced a global crisis far more serious than any previous crises that humanity has experienced. Modern civilization, as a result of its insatiable commitment to profit-making above any other objective, has produced wealth for a small fraction of the world's population while leaving more and more of it in abject poverty. Even the more affluent segments of humanity find themselves living in a polluted environment and engaged in an endless pursuit of consumer products in lieu of satisfaction in their work and in their daily lives.

The development of anthropology is intertwined with the expansion of Western civilization. This prompted one scholar to make the now classic remark that anthropology is the "child of imperialism" (Gough 1968). People in civilized societies, however, have not uncritically accepted the hegemonic ideas of the ruling classes. As noted earlier, two dialectically related traditions of thought began to emerge in the eighteenth century: the prospective, which accepted the development of Western civilization and its dominance over technologically simpler sociocultural systems; and the retrospective, which was more critical of civilization and sensed that its advance results in a loss of community and an increase in social alienation. Although anthropologists have operated within both traditions, our hearts, if not our heads, are frequently in the retrospective tradition. As many of us undoubtedly recognize, "most often, anthropologists have been self-selected, rather marginal persons who have gone in search of that 'common humanity' (Kaplan's phrase) which contemporary Western Civilization . . . has systematically deformed and failed to define except on its own terms" (Diamond, Scholte, and Wolf 1975, 874).

Traditionally, anthropologists expressed their alienation from civilization by focusing their attention almost exclusively upon the supposedly pristine dimensions of primitive societies. The result of this approach was often a description of a small-scale society theoretically existing in virtual isolation from other societies, including colonial and neocolonial powers. Gradually, however, anthropologists were forced to recognize the existence of other populations: peasants, urbanites, ethnic minorities, the poor, and workers in factories and on plantations. Beginning in the 1930s, anthropologists such as Kroeber, Redfield, Warner, Arensberg, and Mead turned their attention to the nature of complex societies or civilizations. Unfortunately, however, while many of these anthropologists saw the positive features of primitive society, they tended to be limited in their critique of civilization and in essence accepted its inevitability. The Boasians, while deeply empathetic toward the Native American cultures they studied, focused almost exclusively on the past history of these cultures and neglected their present plight as "domestic dependents" of the American political economy (Jorgensen, Davis, and Mathews 1978). The studies of African political and kinship systems by the British functionalists often provided colonial administrators with the knowledge needed to carry out a system of "indirect rule."

By regarding civilizations as configurational or ideational systems, some anthropologists—e.g., Boas, Kroeber, Redfield—neglected or minimized their exploitative, stratified, and repressive dimensions. In arguing, for example, that "in civilization the old moral orders suffer, but new states of mind are developed by which the moral order is, to some significant degree, taken in charge," Redfield (1953, 25), although probably not consciously, in effect legitimized the expansionist activities of modern civilization and the capitalist world-system.

Many anthropologists today are reluctant to accept a prospective interpretation of civilization. We are increasingly cognizant that differential power, social stratification, and economic specialization are inherent characteristics of modern civilizations and that from these flow a wide variety of social problems, including abject poverty, alienation from work, racism, crime, the overutilization of the earth's resources, pollution of the natural environment, and the specter of nuclear holocaust. It is my contention that our discipline will have to adopt a retrospective orientation if we are to provide humanity with some of the insights necessary to reverse the destructive trajectory of modern civilization. While it appears that civilization in its multifaceted forms has been an inevitable phase in cultural evolution, our only hope for survival is to work toward an authentically progressive stage. The search for this stage is not new to anthropology, but can be traced back to Morgan's (1964, 467) prediction of a "next higher plane of society," which will involve not only "the termination of a career of which property is the end and aim" but also "a revival, in a higher form, of the liberty, equality and fraternity of the ancient gentes." Almost 100 years later, Leslie White (1973, 65) made a similar prediction by arguing that "if civilization is not destroyed by warfare . . . there will undoubtedly be another political revolution and an entirely new type of society will be established. This new type will most likely be one in which the church-state will be nonexistent: a society in which there will be an administration of *things* rather than the governing of men;

and again society will be organized on the basis of personal relations rather than property relations."

A commitment to improving the world, however, is not a substitute for understanding it. Essential to our comprehension of the world and its diverse peoples is the principle of holism—not the limited holism of the past, which focused on supposedly isolated societies, but one recognizing that indeed we live in a world-system. Furthermore, anthropology cannot simply continue to dwell upon the little peoples of the world—the primitives, the peasants, the proletariats. It must also, as Laura Nader (1972) admonishes us, "study up"—that is, investigate, utilizing whatever means are available to us, the powerful, the rich, and the dominant classes. Only by undertaking such a project will anthropology be able to make the linkages between, on the one hand, transnational corporations, governments, foundations, and think tanks and, on the other hand, the masses of both industrial and Third World nations. Finally, it is important to add that we need to return to "one Enlightenment inheritance that we have lost; the theoretical, instrumental unity of thought and action" (Diamond 1964, 435). This does not mean, however, that we should simply go the way of conventional applied anthropology, which often serves as the handmaiden of the powers that be, but rather that we must make our knowledge available to those peoples who have been the traditional objects of our studies. As Marx (1959, 245) aptly observed, "The philosophers have only *interpreted* the world in various ways; the point, however, is to *change* it."

What Price Civilization? Tuberculosis, for One

ROBERT L. BLAKELY AND DAVID S. MATHEWS

Cultural development in North America was punctuated by episodes of adaptive responses to changing environmental and populational pressures. No response was more dramatic or altered prehistoric lifeways more profoundly than the adoption of agriculture as the primary means of subsistence. Indeed, the advent of food production is often cited as the principal stimulus for the emergence of "civilization" (Braidwood 1964). Increasingly, today, researchers are identifying maladaptive—as well as adaptive—biocultural consequences of the cultivation of crops (see, for example, Robbins 1977, and Perzigian and Widmer 1979). Among the deleterious byproducts of agriculture and the attendant urbanism were heightened incidences of tooth decay, nutritional deficiencies, and infectious diseases such as blastomycosis and tuberculosis (Larsen 1982; Buikstra 1976a).

In this paper we first review evidence from the Old World and the New World for the origin of tuberculosis; we then develop a case for the presence of tuberculosis in the prehistoric southeastern United States; and we close by examining the epidemiological implications of infectious diseases for urbanizing societies.

OLD WORLD VERSUS NEW WORLD ORIGIN

The place of origin of tuberculosis remains hotly debated among anthropologists, epidemiologists, and medical historians (Hooton 1930; Ritchie 1952; Wright and Anderson 1969). That the disease was present in the Old World prior to the voyages of Columbus is not questioned.

Tuberculosis, or "consumption" as it once was called, is well documented in the literature for British Saxons and ancient Greeks and Romans (Morse, Brothwell, and Ucko 1964). And an Egyptian mummy from the Twenty-first Dynasty—a priest of Amûn named Nesperehân—was unmistakably diagnosed as being tubercular (Ruffer 1921). The question is, was the disease also present aboriginally in the New World, or was it introduced to Native Americans by European explorers?

The sources of evidence that can be used to address this question are four: (1) clinical diagnosis of the tubercle bacillus in the soft tissue of mummies from prehistoric America; (2) art and ceramics from aboriginal America depicting individuals seemingly afflicted with tuberculosis; (3) skeletal evidence of tuberculous individuals from pre-Columbian America; and (4) the post-Columbian incidence of tuberculosis among American Indians (a high rate would suggest a lack of prior immunity and therefore the absence of tuberculosis prehistorically).

Unfortunately, the evidence from all four sources is equivocal. Most convincing is a histological study of a prehistoric (Nazca-7 culture) Peruvian mummy that revealed the presence of acid-fast bacilli in the lungs and kidneys (Allison, Mendoza, and Pezzia 1973). Although acid-fast bacilli are responsible for other diseases in humans—leprosy, for example—*Mycobacterium tuberculosis* is the most common such pathogen in humans.

A number of pre-Columbian pottery vessels and works of art seem to depict the hunchback condition characteristic of Pott's disease, or tuberculosis of the spine. Effigy water bottles from the lower Mississippi region display spinal deformities that some consider evidence of tuberculosis (Figure 1). A pictograph from Canyon Hagoe, Arizona, shows hunchback figures playing the flute (Figure 2). Flute playing may indicate recreational therapy (Dubos and Dubos 1952). Webb (1936) regarded the reclining figures as evidence of paralysis of the legs resulting from tubercular involvement of the spinal cord. The phallus on the lower left in figure 2 may indicate spinal irritation. The problem with attributing these spinal deformities to tuberculosis is that a sizable number of other diseases can produce similar conditions. These include actinomycosis, blastomycosis, brucellosis, coccidioidomycosis, echinococcosis, histocytosis, histoplasmosis, malignant tumors, osteitis deformans (Paget's disease), suppurative (pyogenic)

Figure 1. Effigy water bottles from the lower Mississippi region. (Courtesy of the Illinois State Museum and Dan Morse.)

osteomyelitis, rheumatoid arthritis, ankylosing spondylitis (Marie-Strumpell disease), sarcoidosis, Scheuermann's disease, and traumatic arthritis (Buikstra 1976a).

Skeletal evidence of tuberculosis is viewed as inconclusive for the same reason: a number of diseases produce similar spinal deformities. Unlike the individuals portrayed in figures 1 and 2, however, tuber-

Figure 2. Pictograph from Canyon Hagoe, Arizona. (Courtesy of the Illinois State Museum and Dan Morse.)

culosis of the spine commonly produces *angular* kyphosis (hunchback) in the *thoracolumbar* region of the vertebral column. Figure 3, showing a photograph and a radiograph of the vertebral column of a post-contact Caribou Eskimo believed to have been tubercular, illustrates the angular deformity occasioned by anterior erosion of the bodies of the lumbar vertebrae.

In his review of the post-Columbian incidence of tuberculosis among Native Americans, Hrdlička (1909) reported that of 107,000 American Indians examined by physicians at the turn of the century, 1,038 were afflicted with pulmonary tuberculosis, 1,590 had contracted lymph-node tuberculosis, and 208 showed symptoms of bone tuberculosis. These rates, roughly ten times greater than those for the

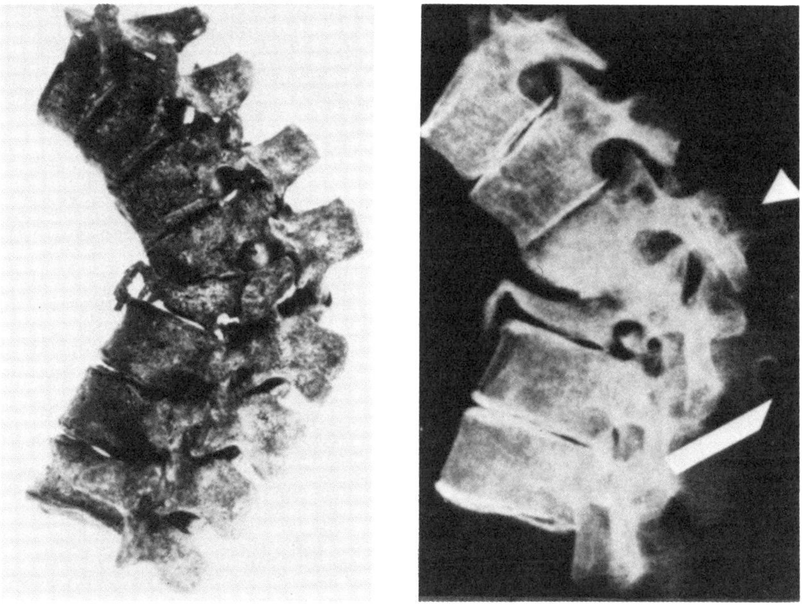

Figure 3. Photograph and radiograph of the angular kyphosis in the thoracolumbar region of a post-contact Caribou Eskimo. On the left are segments T10–L5. Arrows in the radiograph (right) of segments T11–L4 point to abscesses in the spinous processes. (Courtesy of the *American Journal of Physical Anthropology* and Jane Buikstra.)

United States as a whole, suggest to some investigators that Native Americans lacked the immunity that evolution had conferred upon Euro-Americans and Afro-Americans.

Dan Morse (1969), who contends that tuberculosis was not present in pre-Columbian America, has applied Hrdlička's figures to prehistoric skeletal remains. Since roughly 200 out of 100,000 twentieth-century Indians experience bone tuberculosis, Morse reasons that approximately one out of 500 of their prehistoric counterparts should evidence the disease; and he points out that far fewer cases have been even tentatively diagnosed as tuberculous by paleopathologists. The flaw in Morse's logic is that to expect comparable rates of prehistoric and modern tuberculosis, one must assume similar environments. A contagious disease that is supported by crowded and unsanitary conditions might well have been far less prevalent aboriginally—before Indians were forced onto the crowded and unsanitary reservations from which Hrdlička derived his data.

A CASE OF TUBERCULOSIS FROM PREHISTORIC GEORGIA

Of the four sources of evidence for pre-Columbian tuberculosis—acid-fast bacilli in prehistoric American mummies, pre-Columbian figurines purported to depict Pott's disease, prehistoric skeletal lesions attributed to tuberculosis, and a high incidence of tuberculosis among post-Columbian Native Americans—the skeletal evidence has evoked the most controversy (Ritchie 1952; Morse 1969; Buikstra 1981). Paleopathologists may be guilty of arbitrarily assigning discrete skeletal manifestations to diseases that in reality produce overlapping symptoms (Shadomy 1981). How can the anthropologist surmount the problem of diagnosis when different diseases leave similar, or even identical, spinal lesions? One way, according to Buikstra (1976b), is to devise a model of differential diagnosis that takes into account not only the morphology of spinal lesions but also the location of vertebral involvement, other affected skeletal elements, and the epidemiological characteristics and patterning of the disease. Figure 4 reproduces Buikstra's model for the differential diagnosis of spinal pathologies. The following step-by-step observations can diagnose bone tuberculosis (second from the top):

p—observable vertebral pathology;
a1—resorptive (that is, erosive) lesions present;
b1—vertebral involvement characteristic of the disease;
c2—thoracolumbar vertebrae the primary focus;
d3—individuals 12–35 years of age the most likely afflicted;
e1—articular surfaces (that is, bony joints) the site of frequent extra-vertebral involvement (tuberculosis is the only spinal pathology commonly implicating the articular surfaces);
f1—fusion of the vertebrae infrequent except in healing stages.

Buikstra's model of differential diagnosis will be used to identify

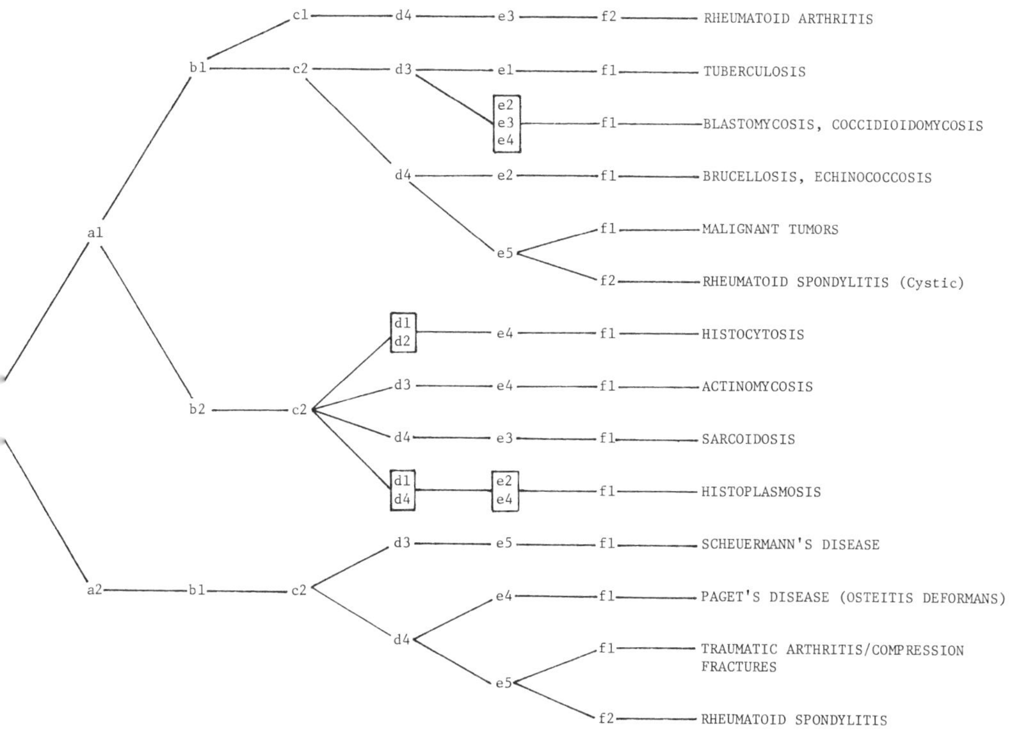

Figure 4. Diagram for the differential diagnosis of spinal pathologies in skeletal remains. Key to variables: (p) common or "root" feature—types of pathology associated with vertebral disease; (a) specific skeletal response—(a1) resorptive lesions present, (a2) resorptive lesions absent; (b) primary locus of skeletal lesions—(b1) vertebral involvement characteristic or common, (b2) vertebral involvement rare; (c) primary foci within spinal column—(c1) cervical, (c2) thoracic/lumbar or nonspecific; (d) age of maximum morbidity/mortality—(d1) birth–3 years, (d2) 3–12 years, (d3) 12–35 years, (d4) 35+ years or age accumulative; (e) site of most frequent extravertebral involvement—(e1) articular surfaces of limb long bones, (e2) diaphyses of limb long bones, (e3) hands and feet, (e4) skull, (e5) nondiagnostic; (f) ankylosis [fusion]—(f1) uncommon except as healing response, (f2) common in primary phase of pathological change. (Adapted from Buikstra 1976b, 359.)

three cases of spinal disease from the Beaverdam Creek site in northeastern Georgia.

The Beaverdam Creek site (9Eb85), located near the confluence of Beaverdam Creek with the Savannah River, consists of a village and badly vandalized mound. Both Savannah II and Lamar components are represented at the site, the former radiocarbon-dated to the thirteenth century A.D. and the latter thought to range from A.D. 1400 to 1600 (Rudolph 1980). Critical to this inquiry is the fact that all three individuals in question can be conclusively assigned to the Savannah II, or *prehistoric,* component.

The first individual (burial 17) is a female who was in her early twenties at the time of death. Despite her relative youth, the lower thoracic and lumbar vertebrae exhibit marked degeneration and collapse. Figure 5, a cranial view of the body of one of the thoracic vertebrae, illustrates the resorptive nature of lesions produced by tuberculosis. Furthermore, the bones evidence the angular kyphosis common—but not confined—to tubercular individuals. Four adjacent thoracic vertebrae are articulated to show an angular deformity of 45° (Figure 6). Two of the lumbar vertebrae were ankylosed (fused), suggesting that the disease may have been in remission (Figure 7). Ankylosis occurs in about 25 percent of all cases of tuberculosis of the spine (Cleveland 1940).

Perhaps most significantly, the articular surfaces of the shoulder and sacroiliac also exhibit pathological involvement. Both have roughened, erosive lesions surrounded by osteoporosis, a condition that often accompanies tubercular degeneration. When these facts are coupled with the age (squarely in the highest-risk group) and even sex (females are more comonly afflicted than males), we feel that a compelling argument can be made for a diagnosis of tuberculosis.

The other two cases of spinal disease from Beaverdam Creek, found in a young adult male (burial 40) and an elderly male (burial 31), were diagnosed as blastomycosis. Blastomycosis is a fungal infection contracted from the soil; hence, it is relatively common among agriculturalists and relatively uncommon among gatherers and hunters (Perzigian and Widmer 1979). Poswell (1976) places the endemic zone for prehistoric blastomycosis within a triangle extending from the Gulf of Mexico to Manitoba to Maine, an area that encompasses virtually all of the eastern woodlands.

Chick et al. (1956) report that in the United States today the disease is far more prevalent among males than females, the higher rate presumably reflecting the males' greater contact with the soil. Given the ethnohistoric evidence that females were at least as active as males in cultivation (Hudson 1976), it would be unreasonable to expect a similar epidemiological pattern in the prehistoric Southeast.

Although blastomycosis and tuberculosis are difficult to distinguish skeletally, *Blastomyces dermatitidis* may leave somewhat smoother resorptive lesions (Furcolow et al. 1966). Moreover, while both affect the thoracolumbar vertebrae, tuberculosis typically produces angular kyphosis, and blastomycosis a rounded deformity. The most frequent sites of extravertebral involvement differ as well: tuberculosis is located in the articular surfaces, and blastomycosis in the long bone diaphyses, where periostitic reaction is not uncommon (Buikstra 1976b). Furthermore, blastomycosis, unlike tuberculosis, is an age-progressive disease, so the elderly can expect to experience greater debility than the young. Furcolow et al. (1966) point out that in the aged the skull and tibia are usually implicated.

The Beaverdam Creek remains exhibit the blastomycosis pattern. The young adult had only vertebral lesions, whereas the elderly male showed—in addition to spinal involvement—lesions on the skull and both tibiae. In figure 8, the striations coursing along the long vertical axis of the bone indicate a periosteal reaction to the disease. The partially healed cut marks running transversely across the anterior aspect of the bone and adjacent to what would have been a soft-tissue infection are interpreted as evidence of surgical procedures designed to relieve the pain and drain pus associated with the disease response.

PALEOEPIDEMIOLOGY AND CIVILIZATION

Two lessons emerge from this study. One tells us that the processes of urbanization that led to "civilization" entailed more than the sociocultural phenomena described in the archaeological and ethnographic literature. Because humans are biocultural organisms, there is a significant biological component to culture change. Disease—like nutrition—is an obvious and appropriate vehicle by which to examine biocultural adaptation, because it stands at the interface between biol-

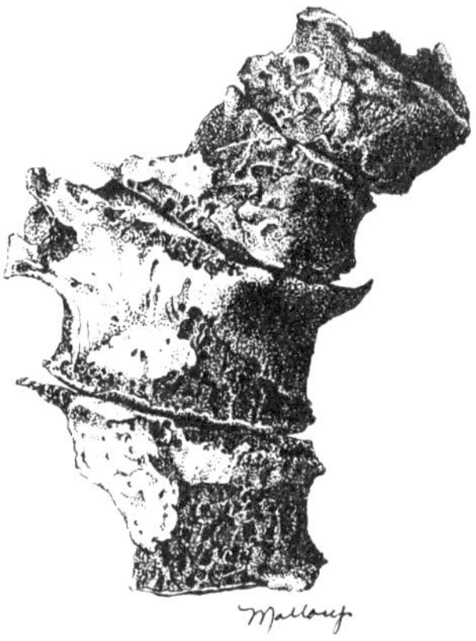

Figure 5. *Left,* cranial view of the body of one of the thoracic vertebrae from burial 17. (Illustration by Marilynn Mallory.)
Figure 6. *Right,* four adjacent thoracic vertebrae from burial 17. (Illustration by Marilynn Mallory.)

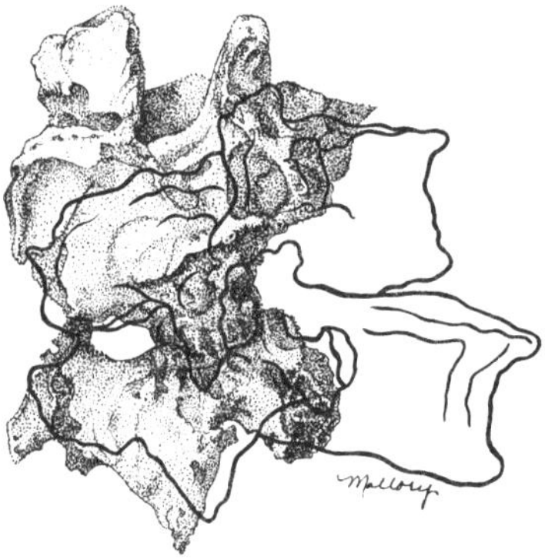

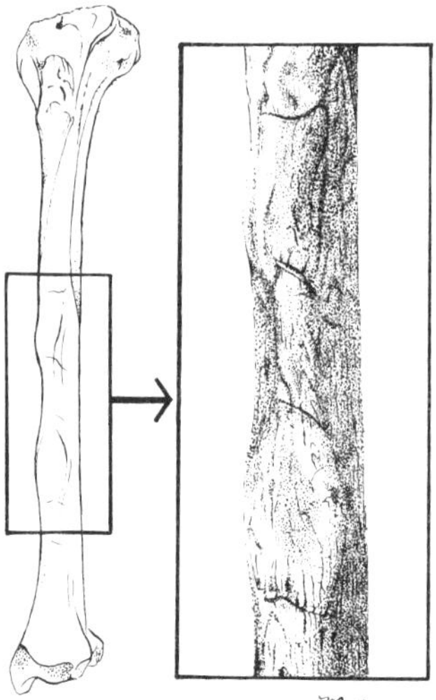

Figure 7. *Left,* two fused lumbar vertebrae from burial 17. (Illustration by Marilynn Mallory.)
Figure 8. *Right,* left tibia of an elderly male from burial 31. (Illustration by Marilynn Mallory.)

ogy, culture, and the natural environment. The other lesson points up the need for biomedical anthropologists—and medical scientists in general—to move beyond the traditional boundaries of symptomatic diagnoses and develop epidemiological models that accommodate biocultural adaptation.

Biomedical anthropologists, particularly paleopathologists, have relied too long on physicians' models of differential diagnosis that are both simplistic and inappropriate. They are *simplistic* because they rarely address more than the morphology and locus of disease symptoms; epidemiological patterning is seldom considered. In the absence of demographic data on age, sex, morbidity, and mortality, paleopathological diagnoses remain little more than reasoned guesses. To achieve greater accuracy, anthropologists must familiarize themselves with the etiology and biobehavior of pathogenic microorganisms and disease vectors—their ecological constraints, reproduction, life cycles, modes of transmission, and parasite/host physiology.

Current models of differential diagnosis are also *inappropriate* for paleopathological research because they are based on modern disease states. Can it be assumed that contemporary diseases have not evolved into markedly different forms from their prehistoric ancestors? We should realize that the pathogenhost relationship is essentially a predator/prey relationship, each selecting for more and more adaptive organisms in the other. As hosts evolve greater immunity, bacteria and viruses must evolve greater virulence. The alternative for both is extinction. Bacterial evolution can proceed faster than human evolution; on the other hand, humans can introduce cultural interventions on their own behalf. The latter fact, however, further complicates paleopathological diagnosis. The clinical diagnoses of today often include the curative effects of Western medical treatments that were not likely to have been practiced in the past (Steinbock 1976). Contemporary clinicians rarely encounter the features common to diseases that have run their course without the intervention of modern medical treatment, including surgery and drug therapy (Buikstra and Cook 1980). In short, we shall continue to misdiagnose prehistoric skeletal lesions if we rely solely on modern clinical evidence of disease.

These limitations are not easily overcome. At least two other sources of epidemiological information can be tapped: (1) historical records—admittedly flawed and ambiguous—offer evidence of disease states and human responses prior to the advent of Western medical technology; and (2) ethnographic accounts provide data on disease actions and non-Western medical practices. Both require that biomedical anthropologists be more demanding of historians, archaeologists, and sociocultural anthropologists.

Given the biocultural nature of adaptive change among humans, it is not surprising that there was a profound biological response to the shift in subsistence from gathering and hunting to food production. Among the deleterious consequences was an increase in the incidence of infectious disease. Since agriculture was an impetus for urbanization, and urbanization a catalyst for "civilization," it is not unreasonable to term such afflictions "diseases of civilization." Although tuberculosis, blastomycosis, and other infectious diseases undoubtedly were present before the advent of food production, the urban environment afforded ideal conditions for their maintenance and transmission.

Until quite recently, such infectious diseases as tuberculosis, scarlet fever, diphtheria, whooping cough, and typhoid fever were the principal killers of city dwellers. At the beginning of the twentieth century, in fact, tuberculosis *still* ranked as the chief cause of death in the United States (Young 1971). It was not until the discovery of the pathogenic nature of bacteria and subsequent development of preventive inoculations that infectious diseases were brought under control in urban America. By 1954, for example, tuberculosis had declined to the eleventh leading cause of death in the United States (Young 1971). Today, in the developed nations, infectious diseases have been largely replaced by new "diseases of civilization": cancer, heart disease, arteriosclerosis, and diseases of the nervous system.

These maladies are different in etiology and mode of transmission from infectious diseases. Does this mean that the study of infectious disease is now relegated to history and paleoanthropology? The answer is no, because, notwithstanding advances in our knowledge and treatment of disease, millions still succumb to infectious diseases annually. Massive programs of preventive inoculation are partial solutions, but cultural prohibitions or economic constraints often diminish their efficacy. These programs also suffer because the developing nations are now urbanizing at rates faster than at any previous time in the world's history.

Infectious disease, while no longer a significant mechanism of population control, continues to exact a toll in human misery and loss of life. Until biomedical anthropologists unravel the coevolutionary relationships between disease states and biocultural adaptation, we shall go on sacrificing human subjects in societal laboratories. It is therefore imperative that we devise predictive epidemiological models in order to further the process of disease eradication. Civilization demands no less.

NOTE

This research was supported, in part, by National Science Foundation grant BNS-8217377. We thank Antoinette B. Brown for her critical reading of an early version of the manuscript; any errors that remain are ours alone. And we gratefully acknowledge the assistance of David J. Hally, who directed the excavation of the Beaverdam Creek site and lent us the skeletons for this study. The illustrations in Figures 5–8 attest to the artistry of Marilynn Mallory.

Paradise Lost, Strayed, and Stolen: Prehistoric Social Devolution in the Southeast

CHRISTOPHER S. PEEBLES

The Mound Builders, according to the received wisdom of the early nineteenth century, were an advanced prehistoric race who, when they disappeared, left no descendants on the North American continent. This myth asserted that the societies that constructed the magnificent earthen edifices, whether Aztecs, Hindus, Danes, or some other ethnic group, were certainly too civilized to be counted as the progenitors of any Indian tribe known to eighteenth- and nineteenth-century historians. Much of this myth of the Mound Builders was demolished in the late nineteenth century by the work of Cyrus Thomas and his associates in the Mound Exploration Bureau of the Smithsonian Institution.[1] They, among others, restored some of the cultural patrimony so crudely denied the native peoples by earlier natural historians.[2]

There is, however, one aspect of the myth of the Mound Builders that has persisted to this day: the notion of their cultural stability, their invincibility. This residual theme contains the belief that because the Mound Builders represented the zenith of cultural development in what is now the eastern United States, only an external force such as the Europeans and their diseases could have caused their destruction. It is a view structurally analogous to the relationship Plato established between his *Republic* and the myth of Atlantis in his *Critias*. According to Plato, social perfection, such as that he adumbrated in the *Republic*, would persist forever if left to its own devices. He invented Atlantis to show that such a society had existed; it was destroyed—and any evidence for it—by earthquakes, volcanic eruptions, and tidal waves. In like manner, although the myth of the Mound Builders has been dispelled, the myth of how they were destroyed lingers on.

Today, the final epoch of mound building in the eastern United States is called the Mississippian. As a whole, the Mississippian spans a period from approximately A.D. 900 to 1600. The truncated pyramidal mounds, one of the characteristics that mark these prehistoric societies as Mississippian, are distributed along major river systems from southern Wisconsin to northern Florida and from eastern Oklahoma to the piedmont of North Carolina.[3] The largest of the Mississippian sites, Cahokia in East St. Louis, Illinois, encompassed more than 100 mounds, covered more than five square miles, and was the center of a political system that blanketed hundreds of square miles;[4] the smallest consisted of a single mound, covered less than one acre, and had a territory of less than twenty square miles.[5]

Recent research has shown that the Mississippian, although embracing many distinct ethnic and linguistic groups, did have a common agricultural adaptation: a focus on a few domesticated plants, chief among them maize, and the exploitation of a very few species of wild animals, all of which were contained within the self-renewing floodplain habitat.[6] Another common thread is social order. Although any measure of social complexity would produce a perceptible spread from most to least complex, Mississippian social organization had at its core a hierarchical arrangement of statuses, offices, and settlements.[7] The zenith of such complexity was reached at different times in different regions, and by the same token, devolution began at different times. Cahokia was at the height of its development in the eleventh century and was well into senescence by the end of the thirteenth.[8] The Natchez of the lower Mississippi Valley can be recognized in the archaeological record as early as the thirteenth century, yet their organization and focus on the temple mound persisted until they were deliberately destroyed by French military action in the mid-eighteenth century.[9] Moundville, in west-central Alabama, which will provide the focus for the remainder of this paper, began its growth in the eleventh and its decline in the mid-fifteenth century. It had collapsed completely by the mid-sixteenth century—either just before or just after the first Spaniards passed nearby on their greedy quest.

The title of this article was chosen as a metaphor for the three distinct stages in the destruction of this pre- and protohistoric Native

American society. Paradise Lost encompasses the autochthonous, prehistoric collapse of Moundville. It covers, albeit roughly, the years from 1450 to 1540. Paradise Strayed, 1540 to 1670, subsumes the sometimes substantial but indirect effects of early Spanish exploration on Native American populations in the region. Paradise Stolen describes the destruction of these populations by European-induced warfare, slave raids, the deerskin trade, and politics. This episode begins sometime before 1680 and ends with the treaties imposed on the remaining Native American groups between 1801 and 1832.

Moundville and its neighboring sites of the Moundville phase are located in a 250-square-mile portion of the Black Warrior River Valley in western Alabama.[10] This particular portion of the valley, which reaches from the Fall Line at Tuscaloosa to the swamps north of Demopolis, is an island oasis of agricultural soils, forests, and oxbow lakes set in a desert of pine barrens. Archaeological research in this area began in 1845 and has continued for 140 years. Five generations of remarkable scholars have made Moundville one of the most systematically investigated Mississippian ceremonial centers in the Southeast (Peebles 1981; Peebles et al. 1981).

Recent research at Moundville and its environs has focused on four aspects of growth and eventual decline: chronology, social organization, economic structure, and adaptation. A combination of ceramic seriation and absolute dating techniques has produced a fivefold chronological scheme (Steponaitis 1981): an Early Mississippian or West Jefferson phase, A.D. 900–1050; a three-part Mature Mississippian or Moundville phase including Moundville I (1050–1250), Moundville II (1250–1400), and Moundville III (1400 to 1500 or 1550); and a protohistoric Alabama River phase, 1500 or 1550 to 1700.[11] Analyses of social organization have examined (1) status in terms of mortuary ceremonialism (Peebles 1974); (2) co-resident groups and activities in terms of residential, industrial, and ritual spaces within communities (Peebles 1979); and (3) the general organization of society in terms of the complexity, size, variety, and location of settlements (Bozeman 1982). Measures of the economy have explored both internal craft specialization and long-distance intersociety exchange. Adaptation has been analyzed through food remains (Scarry 1981b); initial evaluation of the age, sex, and health of the population as manifested in skeletal remains;[12] and trace element analyses of human bone (Peebles and Schoeninger 1981).

Settlements of the West Jefferson phase provided the foundation upon which the Moundville phase grew. Thus far, four sites from this phase have been located: one on the western edge of the Moundville site itself; the others to the north and south. Each is situated on an old river levee, and each is somewhat larger than one acre in size. Nothing in the surface collections from these sites has suggested social or economic differentiation either within or between their populations. Unfortunately, no portion of any of these sites has been excavated; thus there is no information on subsistence activities or on the general health of their populations. If, however, an extrapolation can be made from the West Jefferson phase sites in the upper reaches of the Black Warrior Valley (Jenkins and Nielsen 1974), then these communities were composed of hunter-gatherers who supplemented their diet with domesticated plants, principally maize.

The evidence for the succeeding Moundville I phase, which began approximately A.D. 1050, consists of four sites, each of which had a single truncated pyramidal mound. These single-mound centers were located near earlier villages of the West Jefferson phase, and each had only a very small village area attached to it. Each small settlement, its earthen edifice, and its few permanent residents probably served as the focus for a regional population dispersed among farmsteads and small hamlets.

At this point, Moundville seems to have been merely one of the four single-mound centers, each with its own regional group. Excavations at Moundville show that the narrowly focused Mississippian subsistence base had developed by the beginning of the Moundville I phase (Scarry 1981a and b). Maize provided the bulk of the plant food; deer and turkey provided most of the animal protein. Other aspects of the economic system indicated that the distinction between locally manufactured "coarse" and "fine-ware" ceramic vessels had already been established. In addition, there were a few imported vessels and a very few imported shell and copper artifacts associated with the Moundville I burials at Moundville.

Further analyses of these burials have indicated that approximately 1 percent of the population, all of whom were adults, were interred in places and with items that marked them as having superordinate status.

Again, work with the burials from Moundville indicates that the health of the population was excellent. Of the forty Moundville I phase burials studied, none showed evidence of trauma, chronic disease, or malnutrition.

During the Moundville II phase, A.D. 1200 to 1400, several of the single-mound centers north of Moundville shifted their locations by a mile or so; a new single-mound center was established to the south of Moundville, and more of the population lived in villages rather than being almost completely dispersed in hamlets and farmsteads. Given the increase in the overall number of sites, the total population of the central Black Warrior Valley probably increased as well.

At the beginning of the Moundville II phase, Moundville changed its position of *primus inter pares* to that of *primate,* becoming the central focus for all the other settlements and single-mound centers in the valley. These other sites seem to have been arranged to facilitate control by Moundville and to assure the flow of tribute to Moundville (Steponaitis 1978; Bozeman 1982). Each of the single-mound centers appears to have been the social and economic focus for a "province" or a "region," and each of these territorial subdivisions seems to have had only one single-mound center at any one time.

Moundville's growth in size and power began in approximately A.D. 1200. At this time, three additional mounds were constructed. Their location established the basic bilateral symmetry of the site and began the outline of what would become in the end a 100-acre plaza set in the midst of a 300-acre town. The burial population at Moundville grew fourfold between Moundville I and Moundville II. Moreover, the superordinate stratum of society, at least insofar as burial sociology can be relied upon, grew from 1 percent to approximately 5 percent of the population. Included therein were infants, children, and adults—males and females. There were a few adult males whose grave goods (stone palettes and copper axes), place of burial (in the central part of the mound), and aspects of mortuary ritual (skulls and infant skeletons mixed with their grave fill) suggest that they were the occupants of at least two distinct "political" or "ritual" offices. Of importance is the fact that the occupants of these "offices" were tied to and drawn from the superordinate stratum and not from the bulk of the population.

Despite these social developments, the subsistence sector of the economy did not change between Moundville I and Moundville II. The volume of imported goods increased markedly, however, and some specialization in the production of the "fine-ware" vessels at Moundville occurred. The majority of imported stone, copper, and shell artifacts are found associated with burials of the elite stratum. In contrast, the imported ceramics are found not with the elite but with adult females who were clearly not part of the superordinate group. This distribution suggests that foreign exchange was in the hands of the elite and that lesser items devolved on one segment of the population.[13] As was the case in the Moundville I phase, the health of the Moundville II population seems remarkably good. There is some evidence that the elite stratum may have eaten more meat (Peebles and Schoeninger 1981), but differences in diet were not otherwise marked.

The first half of the Moundville III phase witnessed a continuation and a culmination of the trends that had begun 200 years earlier. New single-mound centers and several large villages were established to the north and south of Moundville. Moundville itself grew to its full size of more than 300 acres, and its population expanded by another 50 percent. Sixteen mounds were constructed, and the whole of the site was enclosed by a palisade.[14] Both the increased nucleation of population in the provinces and the erection of fortifications at Moundville suggest that defense may have become a concern.

By now, if not earlier, the spatial division of statuses and activities had reached their fullest development at Moundville. There were industrial areas where ceramics were fabricated and fired; there were other distinct areas where beads were made, hides were tanned, and maize shucked and shelled. Large "public" buildings stood at the northern corners of the plaza, and "chunkee" yards were nearby to them. A "sweat house" and a "charnel house" were constructed near the southern margin of the plaza; an "elite" residence was segregated from other structures near the extreme northeast border of the site; common residential complexes were situated to the south, east, and west of the plaza.

There were no observable changes in subsistence, no modifications in the system of ranking and prestige, and no major shifts in the health and well-being of the population. Like "Topsy," Moundville "just grew," and by about A.D. 1400, all—at least on the surface—was stable in the central Black Warrior River Valley.

Thus far, Moundville seems to have developed all the classic attributes of a complex chiefdom: hierarchical ranking of settlements, and within settlements hierarchical ranking of persons, statuses, and offices; sumptuary rules and social spaces that separated the elite from the day-to-day activities of society; and an organization and economy that transcended not only households and settlements but the cultural system itself.[15] Moreover, many of the factors that have been proposed to account for the development of chiefdoms seem to have been present at Moundville and in the Moundville phases. Environmental circumscription, the tether of fixed resources, and warfare effectively prevented emigration. As a consequence, a permanent hierarchical organization developed to manage resources and an ever-increasing number of people and social units.[16] The stress on communication and control within this bounded and growing system was reduced and controlled by a permanent pyramid of "offices."[17] Long-distance exchange and local manufacture of durable goods provided the underpinnings and legitimization of such an inegalitarian form of organization. Moundville seems to have been a classic case of a "prestige goods economy" in which knowledge and goods from afar were valued highly, and in which elite manipulation of these goods established control of social obligations. Moreover, this exchange not only satisfied internal needs but also cemented and sustained external alliances.[18]

Within 100 years of reaching its zenith, Moundville was abandoned. The process that led to this event was not presaged either by a decline in the health of the population or by major shifts in the subsistence economy; it was the nonsubsistence sectors of the economy that went into a recession. Sometime after A.D. 1450 the frequency of imported artifacts found with the burials at Moundville declined by more than 75 percent. One of the effects of this depression in foreign exchange was to weaken and ultimately to remove one of the major props that supported the elite. If they were supported through tribute—food and locally manufactured goods—but could not make counter prestations in the form of socially valuable goods, then their legitimacy was called into question.

Several causes can be proposed for the collapse of the external exchange and the prestige goods economy at Moundville, but each currently lacks a proper test. First, given a continuous increase in the population, the volume of surplus available to support the elite and their foreign exchange could have declined. Second, the decline in surplus production could have been exacerbated by the onset of the so-called Little Ice Age around A.D. 1450. Third, access to foreign exchange could have been usurped, either by dissident local elites or by another cultural system altogether. Fourth, the distant societies that supplied Moundville's elite with exotica could themselves have collapsed—their decline coupled through a common cause with that effecting Moundville.

Whatever the causes, the effects of Moundville's collapse were catastrophic. Some single-mound centers may have continued for a time to serve as foci for regional populations, but by the beginning of the seventeenth century, large villages of the Alabama River phase were spaced equidistantly throughout the central Black Warrior River Valley. This spatial arrangement allowed each village to hold and protect the maximum territory. According to available evidence, the population does not seem to have declined markedly between the Moundville phase and the Alabama River phase, but the same evidence suggests that from the later part of the Moundville III phase to the early Alabama River phase, there had been a net out-migration from the central Black Warrior Valley to the central Alabama River Valley.[19]

Social equality, at least equality in death, marked the Alabama River phase. There is little evidence of long-distance trade and no indication that craft production was organized at any level beyond that of the household. The subsistence system underwent *no* major changes: neither additions nor deletions of crops and animals, yet the general health of the population declined precipitously. Two measures of the change in the general well-being of the population can be offered. Whereas fewer than 10 of the 528 individuals examined in one sample of Moundville phase burials showed signs of chronic malnutrition, disease, and trauma, 30 of 66 burials from an Alabama River phase skeletal series showed such anomalies. Perhaps even more telling is a comparison of the ratio of deaths of subadults (twelve to seventeen years of age) to that of adults (more than seventeen years of age).[20] In one sample at Moundville, there were 35 subadults and 404 adults: a ratio of 0.09 to 1. In the Alabama River phase series, there were 8 subadults and 32 adults: a ratio of 0.25 to 1.

Competition for resources leading to malnutrition apparently was the major cause of the increased mortality and the elevated disease load. If, in addition, a greater percentage of the population was engaged in direct agricultural pursuits, increased exposure to soil fungi and other disease vectors may also have been a contributory factor (Powell 1981). Finally, overall adaptation must be taken into account. When the organization provided by Moundville and the satellite centers collapsed, economy of scale, valleywide coordination for defense, and the cooperation that had evened out disparities in production were all lost. If the Moundville phase populations, with their organization, were near the carrying capacity of the valley, then the Alabama River phase populations, without the organization, perhaps found themselves beyond that carrying capacity.

In this way Paradise was Lost.

Let us now turn to the impact of sixteenth-century Spanish exploration on the Southeast in general and on the Alabama River phase populations of the Black Warrior River Valley in particular. Of the early explorers, only Hernando de Soto and his army (and a herd of pigs) reached the interior of the Southeast. They perambulated through the area from 1539 to 1543. Contemporary expert opinion[21] has concluded provisionally that de Soto's expedition may have passed near Moundville but that it did not come into direct, sustained contact with the Alabama River phase populations in the valley.

In 1560, part of Tristán de Luna's army visited Coza, a province on the upper Coosa River. The chief of Coza asked the Spanish commander to aid him in bringing a former vassal group back under his control. The Spanish agreed to the request, and a successful campaign was mounted against the Napochies. Two aspects of this story are of interest here. First, the Napochies seem to have spoken a dialect of Choctaw; the inhabitants of Coza spoke a dialect of Creek. Second, the Napochies may have been located on the Black Warrior River.[22]

From east to west and back again, warfare between the Choctaws and the Creeks apparently has great time depth and has engendered deep feelings in both groups. If exchange and warfare are considered to be two sides of the coin of foreign relations, then there is indirect evidence that this enmity reaches well back into the Moundville phase. Of the 153 imported ceramic vessels found thus far at Moundville, not one can be traced to a source due east of the Black Warrior River. There are vessels from the Nashville Basin and from southeast Missouri; there are vessels from Arkansas and from the Gulf Coast; but there is not a single example from the upper portions of the Coosa, Tallapoosa, and Chattahoochee rivers. Second, when the Carolinians armed the Creeks with guns in the late seventeenth century, the Choctaws were among the first targets the Creeks chose to attack.

I cannot here summarize the recent, excellent work on the cultural geography and ethnohistory of the Southeast. Suffice it to say that this work has transcended the pessimistic prognosis of John Reed Swanton at the conclusion of his monumental book *The Indians of the Southeastern United States:* "Here we lay aside the pen—or rather the typewriter. Though students of culture will still have work to do here [among the documents], the future study of Southeastern Indians rests mainly with the archaeologists" (Swanton 1946, 827). The work of Patricia Galloway, Jeffrey Brain, C. B. Curren, Jr., George Lankford, Chester DePratter, Marvin Smith, and Charles Hudson has been grounded in these same documents, but it has been cross-checked with a keen and critical knowledge of the archaeology of the region. Although the rules that generated the moves of various villages from one valley to another are still far from complete, their work on the protohistoric cultural geography has provided a set of testable locational correlates and transformational sequences for several sixteenth- and seventeenth-century Native American groups in the Southeast.[23] If their several threads of anthropological and historical knowledge are joined, then the descendants of the Moundville phase stand out in even sharper relief: they are, either in whole or in part, the "burial urn cultures" of central and western Alabama.

What is likewise clear, at least in the case of the Black Warrior River Valley communities, is that the transition from superordinate and subordinate settlements and statuses to Hobbesian equality had begun well before the de Soto baseline of 1540. At the time of the earliest Spanish explorations, the Alabama River phase communities already had begun the process of realigning themselves internally and externally. A new social order and a new order of alliances were already emerging. This new social formation was affected by de Soto, de Luna, and Pardo, but they cannot be counted among its causes.

It would be foolish to argue that the Spanish expeditions—or those of other sixteenth-century European explorers, for that matter—had no role in the subsequent developments among the Alabama River phase communities. At the same time, de Soto and his cohorts are not responsible for all the bad things that befell the Native Americans in the whole of the Southeast during the entire span of the sixteenth century. Some groups did succumb to cultural catatonia as a direct result of Spanish depredations; other groups undoubtedly did succumb to the effects of diseases for which Europeans were the vectors. Yet not every group that met the Spaniards during that era was wiped out by disease or reduced to cowering in the woods. It seems likely, as de Soto's chroniclers recorded, that the Vásquez de Ayllón expedition, which landed on the Carolina Coast in 1526, was the cause of the sickness and deaths that struck Cofitachequi, a province located almost 100 miles inland.[24] Yet de Soto found the Apalachee, who had been contacted by the remnants of the Narváez expedition in 1528, vigorous, contentious, and none the worse for wear from their earlier meeting with the Spanish. Moreover, if the subsequent history of the Apalachee is traced, it can be shown that they did not succumb to the effects of visits by de Soto in 1539, by Jesuit priests in 1566, or by the Franciscan friars who lived among them from A.D. 1633 to 1704. It took a combined force of 50 to 100 Europeans and somewhere between 500 and 1,000 Creeks to destroy them early in the eighteenth century.[25]

Yet between A.D. 1500 and 1670, Paradise Strayed.

The remainder of the story is a bit sordid. The Colony of Carolina was chartered in 1663, and Charlestown was founded in 1670. The lords proprietors expected their colony to be an extension of manorial England, filled with nobility and stout yeomanry. Instead they got the "Goose Creek Men": Henry Woodward and Thomas Nairn, James Moore and his friend Colonel Chicken. These men were mercantilists and Indian traders. To them the Indian trade was an outlet for cheap merchandise and a source of deerskins and Indian slaves. Their branding irons marked both—skins and slaves.[26]

To serve the ends of trade, the Goose Creek Men armed the Savannahs, who then destroyed the Westos in 1680. They then armed the "Tallapoosies," who ranged far and wide, and Emperor Brim of the Cowetas was—at least initially—their creation and lackey. By 1690 the Creek towns, allied with the Carolinians, had cleaned out the central Black Warrior Valley; by 1702, when Bienville armed the Choctaws, he noted that over several decades their bows and arrows had not been very effective against Creek guns (Bienville [1726] in Rowland and Sanders 1932, 499–702).

Their lordships, the proprietors of Carolina, took a dim view of the trade in Indian slaves. As early as 1685 they wrote to their agent, "[Do] not appoint Mr. Maurice Mathews, Mr. James More or Mr. Arthur Midleton whom Wee have removed from being so for disobeying our orders in sending away the Indians for wee would not have those men or their abetters Imployed in any office" (Salley 1929, 28). Eight years later they wrote: "We are of the opinion that ye Goos-creek men have been enabled to draw many evil minded men to side with them in keeping things unsettled out of hopes thereby to avoid paying Us our rents" (Salley 1931, 111). Thomas Nairn, a Goose Creek man to the core, countered in 1708 with what had been his position from the beginning:

> Our friends at Talopoosies and Chicasas Imploy Themselves in making slaves of such Indians about the Lower parts of the Mississipi as are now subject to the french. The good prices the English Traders give them for slaves Encourage them to this trade Extreamly and some men think it serves to Lessen their number before the French can arm them and it is a more Effectuall way of Civilising and Instructing Then all the Efforts used by the French Missionaires. (Salley 1947, 197)

It was a long way from London to Charlestown and perhaps, at least symbolically, nearly as far from the Governor's Mansion in Charlestown to Goose Creek. No matter the justification—European feuds, religious antagonisms, or pure economics—the Goose Creek men recognized that deerskins and Indian slaves were the currency that bought the colony's imports.

In sum, economic forces and population dynamics in the Southeast of the late seventeenth century can be seen as three oblique vectors: Europeans, especially in the form of traders and trading posts; Native American populations; and the density and distribution of deer. Deer and humans competed for territory. Humans competed with other humans for deer. Both humans and deer could be converted into cash and other goods by traders. Traders wanted control over the humans who could hunt deer and enslave other humans. When these three vectors are resolved, the solution—at least its graphical representation—yields a series of vortices. Each vortex comprises a Native American population that swirled slowly across some part of the Southeast. Much like the tornadoes seen in animated cartoons, they swept across uninhabited territory, vacuuming up deer and any stray humans who happened to be in the way. As one vortex came near to another, if they were of roughly equal size, they repelled each other; but if one was markedly larger, it swallowed the smaller. The product of this conquest was deer and slaves as well as additional territory to support deer. Just as there was mutual attraction and repulsion among populations, deer herds, and hunting territory, so each population was either attracted to or repelled by one or more of the European powers and their traders and trade goods. The shifting, unstable values for each of these three vectors finally yielded the configuration of Native American populations across the face of the Southeast at the time of the American Revolution: the Five Civilized Tribes.[27]

The magnitudes that can be assigned to these vectors are staggering. Between 1680 and 1720 an average of 50,000 deerskins and 500 Indian slaves passed through Carolina per year. In the peak years, more than 120,000 skins were shipped (1707) and more than 4,000 Indian slaves acknowledged (1703, as the result of the destruction of the Apalachee). Thus, conservative totals—ignoring deer that were killed for food or that had less than prime pelts, and Native Americans killed outright and thereby rendered unfit to be slaves—comprise at least 20,000 humans and 2,000,000 deer in a span of forty years.[28]

On eighteenth-century maps the Black Warrior River Valley generally is shown as "quite uninhabited." As late as 1800 both the Creek and the Choctaw claimed it, and fought a war over their claims at the beginning of the nineteenth century. They first agreed to play a ball game, the winner to get all the land between the Black Warrior and the Tombigbee rivers. The ball game ended in a dispute, however, and the dispute escalated into armed conflict. The Choctaws won the first round; the Creeks returned the next fall to continue the fight; and the Choctaws eventually won the second battle, but only after calling up reinforcements (Cushman 1899, 184–93).

The newly independent United States began to remove the Native Peoples of Alabama as soon as they had consolidated their power in the Old Southwest. The Choctaws of the central Tombigbee were among the first to go. The land between the rivers was ceded to the United

States by the Choctaws in the Treaty of St. Stephens in 1816 (Debo 1934; DeRosier 1970).

And so Paradise was Stolen.

NOTES

Thanks are due my colleagues at the University of Alabama, the Institute of Pre- and Protohistory, University of Amsterdam, and Indiana University. The notes and bibliography that follow go only a small way in the accounting of my debts to members of the Moundville Project: Vincas Steponaitis, Margaret Schoeninger, C. Margaret Scarry, Tandy K. Bozeman, Paul Welch, Margaret Hardin, Sander van der Leeuw, and James B. Griffin. Special thanks are due to Patricia Galloway for her intelligence and friendship and to C. B. "Sonny" Curren and Vernon Knight for answering my never-ending stream of questions. As always, I offer my gratitude to David Hoyd DeJarnette, teacher and friend. My research at Moundville has been supported by the National Science Foundation (GS2837 and BNS 78-07133-01); my thanks go to the Director and Associate Director of the Anthropology Program, Drs. John Yellen and Mary Greene.

1. See, for example, the first two chapters of *A History of American Archaeology* (Willey and Sabloff 1980). See also Thomas's major syntheses (1894) of the work of the Mound Exploration Bureau.

2. Henry Savage (1979) gives an extended description of the tenets held by the "Natural History School" of scholarship. Various members of this "school" went to great lengths to attribute all evidence of substantive prehistoric cultural accomplishments by Native North Americans either to immigrants from the Old World (the Ten Lost Tribes, etc.) or to refugees from the High Civilizations of Mesoamerica.

3. These general boundaries are taken from Griffin (1967). Despite the fact that his article is almost twenty years old, it is still the best short summary of the prehistory of the eastern United States.

4. The best general summary for Cahokia is by Fowler (1974). A critical overview is provided in an unpublished paper by Hall (1975). An exuberant, wide-ranging report of recent work in Cahokia's environs can be found in Bareis and Porter (1984).

5. See, for example, work in the Lubbub Creek archaeological locality in west central Alabama (Peebles 1983) and the final report of the Powers phase research in southeast Missouri (Price and Griffin 1979).

6. The best synthesis of Mississippian human ecology is found in Smith (1978), especially in the summary.

7. Compare, for example, Peebles and Kus (1977); Brown (1971); and Black (1979).

8. The decline and demise of Cahokia is explained in detail by Hall (1980).

9. Swanton (1911); Steponaitis (1981b).

10. Background material can be found in a series of papers by Christopher Peebles, Paul D. Welch, Tandy K. Bozeman, C. Margaret Scarry, Lauren Michals, Peebles and Margaret Schoeninger, Alice Haddy and Albert Hanson, Vincas Steponaitis, Sander van der Leeuw, and Margaret Hardin in *Southeastern Archaeological Conference Bulletin 24* (1981). The reference list appended to these articles includes most of the recent published and unpublished research on Moundville.

11. This fivefold division is cast in the cultural-historical terms commonly used by Southeastern prehistorians. In the case at hand, "phase" can be replaced with "period" without loss of meaning. For a complete exposition of Moundville's chronology see Steponaitis (1981a).

12. Data for Moundville and Alabama River phase skeletal series come from three unpublished sources: (a) an analysis of ca. 700 skeletons from the Moundville site by Margaret Schoeninger, Clark Larsen, and Christopher Peebles; (b) an unpublished M.A. thesis by Mary Cassandra Hill (1979); and (c) an unpublished paper by Mary Lucas Powell (1981). Powell and Hill are currently engaged in analyses of the complete skeletal series from Moundville for their doctoral dissertations at Northwestern University and the University of Massachusetts, Amherst, respectively.

13. James B. Griffin, when told of this particular association of imported vessels with adult female burials, suggested that these individuals may have been in-marrying women who brought the vessels with them from their homelands. This is a reasonable conjecture, although it will prove hard (but not impossible) to test.

14. Moundville may have been fortified at an earlier date, but thus far there is no evidence of palisade lines from either Moundville I or II deposits. The final Moundville III walls outline and enclose Moundville at the limits of its growth.

15. There are several excellent summaries of the archaeology of chiefdoms. Among the most literate and thoughtful are Renfrew (1979a, 1979b) and Earle (1978).

16. The relationships among various kinds of environmental "stress" and the development of social complexity can be found, for example, in Carneiro (1981b), Gilman (1981), and Peebles and Kus (1977).

17. See especially the work of Gregory Johnson and Henry T. Wright III: Wright (1983, 1977), Wright and Johnson (1975), and Johnson (1982).

18. The clearest expositions of the notion of a "prestige goods economy" can be found in Wright (1983) and Frankenstein and Rowlands (1978). Somewhat more opaque discussions are provided by Friedman (1979, 1982) and Rowlands (1982), as well as in several articles in a book edited by Friedman and Rowlands (1977). Elegant ethnographic analyses of the relationships between prestige, social rank, possession of highly valued material goods, and control of access to information can be found in the work of Helms (1979) on Panamanian chiefdoms, and in Douglas and Isherwood's (1978) essay on contemporary preindustrial and industrial economies.

19. The fundamental monographs on the Alabama River phase are unpublished; they are Sheldon (1974), Curren and Little (1981), and Hill (1979). Additional primary descriptive materials were published in the 1920s in *Arrowpoints* by Peter Brannon and his associates. Copies of this journal are found in only a very few public and private libraries today.

20. This comparison eliminates the underrepresentation of infants and children in archaeological samples of human remains. It includes only individuals who have made it past weaning and survived the usual set of childhood diseases, and who should have had a good chance of reaching adulthood. The data for these comparisons are taken from Schoeninger, Larsen, and Peebles (unpublished field notes) and Hill (1979).

21. When these lines were first written, in 1982, Cailup B. Curren, Jr., agreed with their substance; they were in accord with his written report of a year before (Curren and Little 1981). Recently, however, he seems to have modified his views (Curren 1982). He now allows the possibility that the de Soto expedition may have had a role in the collapse of Moundville and that the Alabama River phase communities of the Black Warrior River Valley represented the ultimate seventeenth-century product of this collapse.

22. The location of the Napochies was fixed by John R. Swanton (1922, 230–40). Vernon J. Knight, Jr., however, in a recent conversation, suggested that given the recent revisions in the supposed location of Coza (Curren, Little, and Lankford 1981) the Napochies may have lived in the Tennessee River Valley rather than the Black Warrior.

23. Galloway (1981); Curren, Little, and Lankford (1982); Hudson, Smith, and DePratter (1984).

24. I do not believe that the wholesale application of disease as an explanatory factor for cultural change in the protohistoric Southeast can be sustained. Yet, as George R. Milner (1981) points out in his closely reasoned article, it is a testable proposition in each instance.

25. The destruction of the Apalachee is described in Swanton (1922) and in Boyd, Smith, and Griffin (1951). Recent work by John Scarry and his associates (Scarry 1984; Scarry and Payne 1981; Payne 1982) gives an up-to-date summary of archaeological research in the Red Hills region of northwest Florida.

26. I am indebted to J. Leitch Wright (1981) not only for the appellation "the Goose Creek Men" but for much of the substance of my discussion of Indian slavery and European mercantilism. As far as I know, the first anthropologist to recognize the importance of Indian slavery for the protohistory and early history of the Southeast was Charles Hudson (1976). Other works on Indian slavery include Snell (1972), P. Brown (1975), Lauber (1913), and Crane (1929).

27. James B. Griffin (1967) noted the "pull" of trading posts and factories in the early historic period. James A. Brown (1975) has assessed the overall impact of the Europeans on the Native Americans. The most thoughtful discussions of the deerskin trade are to be found in Crane (1929) and especially in Waselkov (1978).

28. I developed these figures from Crane (1929, 110–12), and Snell (1972, 126).

Population Centers at Risk: Stability and Stress

EDWARD L. GREENAMYRE

A review of the cultural record from protohistoric to contemporary times reveals that catastrophes are as ancient as the earliest emergence of compact residence patterns, since the initially slow yet relentless human tendency toward greater population concentrations has progressively increased the potential for large-scale loss of life and property during periods of collective emergency. As the nomadic hunting and gathering practices of the Paleolithic and Mesolithic ages gave way to sedentary Neolithic agricultural settlements, the stage was set for higher casualty tolls whenever disasters subsequently struck. The advance of industrial urbanism throughout the world over the past two centuries has continued this earlier trend. It has also produced something of an ironic demographic *non sequitur* by fostering generally unprecedented levels of community growth and at the same time undermining the utility of the extended families, lineages, and clans around which traditional and more personally immediate concepts of social unity coalesced.

It is now evident that human reactions involving pronounced psychic distress have been a persistent and harmful byproduct of catastrophic events, whatever their degree of antiquity. Ecological difficulties accompanied by widespread and severe anxiety are seen as important factors in the collapse of impressive civilization centers, such as Mohenjo-daro and Harappa in the Indus Valley (Chard 1969, 249–54; Fagan 1983, 319–28; Wheeler 1968, 126–31). In later times massive psychological trauma, occasioned by what appears to have been a particularly virulent form of scarlet fever having its origin in Ethiopia, cut short the Greek "Golden Age" and, in 404 B.C., contributed to the defeat of Athens by Sparta in the Peloponnesian War. The destruction of the Roman Empire as a potent force in world affairs in the fifth century A.D. was not caused simply by outbreaks of malaria, bubonic plague, and possibly smallpox among its inhabitants, or by anthrax epidemics in livestock herds; the population was still sufficiently dense to maintain a formidable standing army. The principal factors that brought about the Roman downfall included the demoralization that accompanied the sporadic appearance of these diseases, and the myriad social problems that were either generated or exacerbated by them (Cartwright with Biddiss 1972, 6–27; McNeill 1976, 105–20). In the New World, a damaged collective will, induced by the physical effects of an increasingly unstable food supply, seems to have figured importantly in the demise of the Mayan centers of culture in Mesoamerica (Cowgill 1964; Howells et al. 1940; Saul 1972).

These facts, as well as a continuing accumulation of more recent sociocultural data, have established that all disasters carry serious psychological implications. Further, it is evident that the likelihood of shared psychic injury must be given the proper degree of attention if the incidents themselves are to be adequately understood and properly administered. Among anthropologists, Wallace and his colleagues have been instrumental in focusing scrutiny upon the cross-cultural continuity of elements promoting anxiety within threatened communities (Wallace 1956; Demerath and Wallace 1957).

Mental trauma does not depend for its existence solely upon the fall of empires or the destruction of entire urban areas. Severe personality disorders of a transient or even chronic nature can be engendered by a sequence of events affecting a relatively small social unit—a family, residents of a certain hotel, patrons of a particular theater, or even a single person under excessive stress: textbooks of abnormal psychology are filled with cases in which an aspect of the physical or cultural environment impinges upon only one individual and results in grave behavioral aberrations. The residual consequences of even these initially isolated situations can, in turn, touch the lives of many citizens, a number of whom may well be beyond the victim's kin group or circle of acquaintances. Thus, such problems are rarely completely private. Even gradual changes in a person's way of living or social status have been shown to increase the chance of physical and mental health difficulties (Pelletier 1977). If, as is the case with disasters, these changes are compressed into a short period of time and accompanied by tragedy, Harshbarger (1974, 56) correctly asserts that such probabilities increase dramatically.

As Coleman (1976, 116–18) has observed, "Stress can be expensive." Stress may well reduce individual flexibility in thought and action with respect both to a specific set of disruptive circumstances and to conditions within the more general physical and social environment. Often those who seem to be performing well in demanding situations, even over extended periods of time, may be doing so by sacrificing the inherent reservoir of resilience necessary to sustain other facets of their existence. A case in point would be the law enforcement officer who appears to be satisfactorily adjusted to the strains of a protracted and rigorous assignment, but who uncharacteristically falls victim to a low-grade infection, becomes visibly less able to cope with reasonably routine marital pressures, or begins to exhibit an increasing dependence upon alcohol (Kroes 1976; Terry 1981). Finally, contrary to popular belief, rest does not completely restore victims of stress. Each severely taxing experience uses up what Selye (1956, 274–75) has called "reserves of adaptability" that can never be fully replaced.

Pioneer efforts to develop a clinical understanding of the relationship between human exposure to calamity and the resulting psychological trauma were undertaken within our own society at least as early as four decades ago, when studies were made of victims of the 1942 Cocoanut Grove nightclub fire in Boston and their families (Adler 1943; Lindermann 1944). Only during the past few years, however, have organized attempts to provide effective crisis therapy become a fundamental part of more enlightened disaster relief programs. In a 1965 symposium held by the American Association for the Advancement of Science to discuss the most feasible approach to civil emergency preparedness in the event of military conflict, only limited attention was given to the inherent psychiatric problems attending a catastrophe. A segment dealing with disaster-related medical considerations was devoted almost entirely to restoring the physical well-being of victims through proper treatment of burns, radiation sickness, and the effects of various bacteriological agents. The complicating factor of psychological trauma was acknowledged only to the extent of noting that severe mental distress can be experienced by those who suffer loss of loved ones or who are assigned to extended service on mass burial details (Sidel 1966).

The fact that the current federal Disaster Relief Act (Public Law 93-288, May 22, 1974) and its more recent amendments authorize the President to make funds available for crisis intervention in time of emergency indicates a slowly growing awareness of the necessity for civil and relief agencies to respond to the mental health needs of populations at risk. Yet a requirement of this nature is not fulfilled simply by recognizing its existence. While lay persons receiving competent direction can often make substantial contributions to crisis therapy, one must avoid the mistaken assumption that symptom identification and treatment are merely "commonsense" undertakings that can be performed by any normally intelligent person. Perhaps the situation is best understood through a comparison with more conventional forms of first aid. Bystanders can be of considerable assistance to a physically injured person if they have been exposed to even the most abbreviated course of training, but they can greatly aggravate the victim's condition, through either overt action or neglect, when guided by whim or intuition alone.

If all those having either a marginal or total inability to cope with crisis-producing events reacted in exactly the same way, it would be a relatively simple matter to prepare an abridged list of "danger signals" and appropriate therapeutic procedures to be followed by recovery personnel. Unfortunately, the way in which a particular situation is perceived and the emotional reaction to it can vary significantly from person to person (Schulberg 1974). It is for this reason that individuals with some experience in detecting psychic trauma are required at the scene of an emergency if relief organizations are to develop an accurate assessment of the extent to which such trauma is present.

I will briefly review three specific disasters of varying degrees of magnitude, and search for common characteristics that can be of value in any attempt to develop a program of crisis intervention.

The exceptionally destructive tornado that struck Xenia, Ohio, on April 3, 1974, was the most serious of sixty similar incidents that took place in an eleven-state area, resulting in a total of 266 deaths and property damage in excess of $365 million. In Xenia alone, 33 people died, 1,200 persons were injured, and approximately half of the public and private structures lying in the sixteen-mile path of the storm were destroyed. These included the high school, both junior high schools, and many of the facilities at Central State University in nearby Wilberforce. Winds of a velocity at times exceeding 300 miles per hour are reported to have pulled canceled checks from storage cabinets in a local building and sent them drifting earthward 200 miles away (Ohio

State University Disaster Research Center 1975a; Schanche 1974, 16–19). In spite of the storm's intensity, however, the great majority of residents escaped harm, and most still had their property intact. Yet few were left untouched by the residual psychological repercussions of the event.

Symptoms common among direct victims included an increase in anxiety reactions, feelings of depression and anger, and a greatly diminished capacity to cope with the circumstances in which they found themselves. Members of the community not harmed by the storm and suffering no property losses often became "indirect" victims, exhibiting pronounced symptoms of guilt because they had escaped when many relatives and close friends had not (Schanche 1974, 61). Nine years of experience as a consultant to the Tennessee Emergency Management Agency on disaster planning and recovery operations procedures has convinced me that such reactions can persist in a sustained form, in spite of the fact that those so afflicted are in most cases intellectually aware that they could have done nothing to assist the persons who were injured or killed.

Subsequent investigation of the Xenia tornado and its aftermath uncovered a number of important facts relevant to any effort to formulate crisis therapy procedures. First, there was a greater requirement for mental health services in the broader sense than was indicated by expressed need; one could not obtain an accurate picture of the situation simply by keeping records of those direct and indirect victims who voluntarily sought this form of assistance (Ohio State University Disaster Research Center 1975b). Factors contributing to this state of affairs typically include ignorance on the part of survivors concerning available aid, fear that they might be labeled "mentally ill," and an inadequate ability among line relief and recovery personnel to recognize psychological stress reactions. Therefore, second, it was concluded that most of the response to any phase of a disaster must be delineated before its actual impact. While programs should be flexible and make use of all possible local resources, they cannot be based simply on random and unsystematic attempts to react to on-site emergencies as they arise. Further, any plan should make provisions for servicing the needs of those most likely to be neglected in times of collective stress: indirect victims, the aged, and the caregivers themselves (Ohio State University Disaster Research Center, undated). Members of this last group, who are quite vulnerable to emotional pressures stimulated by their exposure to the wider implications of severe community crisis and their own possible personal losses from it, can easily become an invisible part of the recovery landscape in the absence of sufficient supervisory sensitivity.

One significant feature of catastrophes or acute emergencies is that problems existing prior to their arrival do not simply dissolve as the affected individual or family finds new strength in adversity (Schanche 1974, 64). Sometimes there is the short-range appearance of such a phenomenon, but in the longer term, the new hardships (death of relatives and friends, loss of home or business, destruction of valued personal possessions, evaporation of savings) simply overlie older ones and place even more stress on those involved. Previous strains related to job or marriage do not generally go away but surface again in perhaps an even more bitter and antagonistic form.

Another disastrous event of recent years was the extensively reported collapse of a slag dam near Buffalo Creek in southern West Virginia on February 26, 1972. The rupture of the dam wall released the contents of a fourteen-acre lake containing 132 million gallons of water mixed with waste traceable to a nearby coal processing plant. This amalgam, in the form of a thirty-foot-high wave, descended on the valley below. The direct results of the inundation were 125 persons dead, 4,000 residents (four-fifths of the local population) homeless, and $50 million in property damage (Caudill 1972; Stern 1976).

While the immediate effects were, as in most disasters, clearly evident, Gleser, Green, and Winget (1981) have established through their in-depth examination of regional psychosocial consequences that the long-range human costs have been more subtle and difficult to determine. Entire communities situated along the creek, which emptied downstream into the Guyandotte River, were destroyed. There were the usual problems with grief and guilt management following the flood, but there were also increased fears of thunderstorms, a generally manifested inability to sleep, eating problems, excessive concern over bodily functions, and memory difficulties among both adults and children. Church (1974, 61–62), who gave considerable personal attention to this disaster, observed that the psychological distress visible in each of these two basic age groups could at times be mutually reinforcing. Blaufarb and Levine (1972, 17–18) found a similar communication of anxieties between parents and children following an earthquake in the San Fernando Valley of California.

A number of actions taken by Buffalo Creek area relief agencies, though motivated by good intentions and a desire to provide a rapid response to the emergency, contributed to the stress already being imposed upon afflicted residents. Displaced families were placed haphazardly in densely packed trailer parks without regard to old community groupings; survivors were ignored when decisions were made that affected their welfare. As a result, resentment and hostility developed, depressions deepened, anxiety reactions became more evident, and there was a clear loss of initiative on the part of the victims. These conditions gave rise to subsequent recommendations by investigators that natural community alliances among surviving friends and neighbors should be maintained in temporary shelters to the maximum possible extent, and that a spokesperson should be selected to represent survivor groups in their dealings with officials responsible for relief operations. It was further suggested that persons charged with disaster recovery duties receive ongoing training in methods for dealing with the emotional impact of such events. Persistent emphasis was also placed on the need for better crisis intervention planning if victims of future catastrophes were to receive appropriate mental health services from the state (Church 1974, 61–63; Kerns 1976; West Virginia Department of Mental Health, undated).

One significant psychological aspect of the Buffalo Creek incident should be of interest to anyone developing mental health intervention plans in regions whose residents hold strong fundamentalist religious beliefs. As Kästenbaum (1974, 69) indicates, disasters throughout history have been interpreted as events having moral significance. Generally, as in the Christian Bible, they have been assumed to reflect the wrath of a deity at either improper collective behavior or neglect of ritual responsibilities. In the aftermath of the tragic events at Buffalo Creek, some survivors, viewing the devastation around them as "God's will," believed the resentment and distress they felt to be somehow sinful. The situation was thus made more traumatic for them, since they felt obliged to suppress the need to ventilate their inner feelings. Local ministers performed a valuable service by persuading many of those bearing the dual burden of great loss and religious guilt that their anxieties were normal under the circumstances.

This and additional evidence supports the contention that, both because of their experience and the community respect they enjoy, ministers should be systematically incorporated into crisis intervention activities. The quality of trust must not be underestimated, as it often permits local religious leaders to validate the legitimacy of a stranger to wary residents in remote locations, and the worthwhile nature of the activities in which he or she is engaged (Kerns 1976).

Some veteran observers of the West Virginia economic and political scene have privately suggested that concerns expressed by area inhabitants over the possibility of divine intervention at Buffalo Creek were rooted less in the prevailing value system than in cynical attempts by influential outsiders to promulgate an explanation that would diminish their own level of accountability. There can be little doubt that general acceptance of such a postulate would be congenial to anyone wishing to avoid more secular interpretations of legal liability. Yet as a native son of the geographical region involved, I can affirm that a traditional religious outlook strongly influenced by Old Testament views with respect to the wages of sin far predates this particular catastrophe and does not flow simply from some Machiavellian manipulation of the citizenry by representatives of either the state government or indigenous mining interests.

In a similar instance reported from Xenia, members of an eighth-grade class exhibited a high degree of excitement and distress when it was suggested that the destruction of a mostly black neighborhood was the result of "God's judgment" (Schanche 1974, 63–64). Again, the value of prompt constructive action by a clergyman in dispelling irrational assumptions of this type is quite evident.

To conclude our brief community disaster survey, we will examine an unusual incident spawned by an unfortunate synthesis of locally atypical environmental circumstances. This particular emergency approached the Xenia disaster in total damage costs but did not contribute to loss of life. It might be expected that substantially fewer psychological stresses would develop under these conditions, yet this did not prove to be the case. On June 16, 1965, a tornado striking forty miles south of Denver, Colorado, deposited three to five inches of rain at a time when feeder streams serving the South Platte River, which flows through the city, were already full from three days of continuous precipitation. As a result, a twenty-foot-high wall of water passed through

Denver's metropolitan area and left behind $325 million in property damage. Unlike many flood situations, this one had a number of uncommon features: it was sudden and unexpected (in this respect it compares with Buffalo Creek); it struck a population unaccustomed to such a threat; it resulted in highly localized damage. No lives were lost, because a Douglas County sheriff issued a timely warning to authorities when he saw the massive body of water forming and realized the direction it would eventually take; as a result, 3,700 families were evacuated to safety as a precautionary measure (Drabek and Stephenson 1971, 187–89).

Although the postflood inquiry did not delve deeply into the need for crisis intervention activities in Denver, several findings did have ramifications important to the formulation of more effective and broadly based mental health policies for periods of collective stress. Drabek and Stephenson (1971, 196–200) noted, for example, that members of separated families facing the emergency felt more acute pressures than did those with the kin unit intact. These investigators again emphasized, therefore, that early family reunification is a critical step in reducing potentially serious psychic distress among residents of any threatened community. Such a program also makes things less difficult for authorities trying to maintain a smoothly functioning emergency operation. Persons separated from their loved ones have proved likely to engage in illegal acts, ignore regulations, and behave in ways inimical to their own and others' safety when attempting to locate individuals who are important to them.

It is now evident that traumatic psychological pressures accompany all disasters and exert considerable influence over both the survivors and those associated with them. The cases chosen for discussion demonstrate that anxieties often begin with the initial warning and build in intensity until the stressful events have run their course. In some instances, emotional damage continues to accrue long after any physical effects have ceased to be felt. It can be anticipated, then, that a disaster will initiate, as well as aggravate, mental illness, since both well-adjusted and previously disturbed community members will be its victims (Kinston and Rosser 1974, 450–51). Further, the earlier a crisis intervention program can be initiated, the greater the chances for reducing the frequency and intensity of subsequent emotional difficulties (Tuckman 1973, 151). As Coleman (1976, 208) has documented, the prompt application of mild reassurance therapy, ventilation of reactions to traumatic experiences, and proper rest can alleviate the symptoms of most civilian shock reactions.

In view of the facts we have examined, it becomes appropriate to wonder why the psychic needs of those who are injured or in desperate circumstances are so often overlooked. One reason seems to be that the problem (or presumed lack of it) is in the eye of the beholder. Behavioral scientists have observed that the traumatized individual, regardless of his or her symptoms, is often in a "no win" situation. Neurosis and disorientation are such constant companions of both the threat and reality of physical injury that even medical professionals offering treatment are conditioned to consider it normal and unworthy of serious clinical consideration (Titchener 1970). On the other hand, the person with less striking symptoms is also overlooked. Disaster workers with their hands full are often appreciative of the quiet and tractable individual who, unlike more excited and angry survivors, is almost mechanically obedient to their directions. These persons, too, as Schulberg (1974, 85) observes, run the risk of being ignored. Both those who are visibly distressed and those who are nonreactive, then, may need psychiatric attention, but personnel charged with on-site relief responsibilities will not consistently apprehend this possibility.

Even experienced conventional care-givers tend to recognize a need for crisis intervention only when a victim's actions become truly bizarre. Flagrantly irresponsible discharge of firearms, attempted self-destruction, or panic are seen as obvious indications that a subject requires the attention of a therapist. More subtle anomalies of behavior, though equally suggestive to the experienced mental health specialist, are not generally perceived as signals of trauma.

As earlier studies by Quarantelli (1954; 1960), Schultz (1964), and Wolfenstein (1957) have shown, however, these grossly demonstrative characteristics are seldom present in even the most threatening of emergencies. In fact, those caught in the grip of collective adversity have been found to exhibit a genuine sense of concern for their fellow sufferers, and to act in a manner that must be termed commendable by any standard. Observers are constantly impressed by the resourceful and selfless behavior found at disaster scenes (Fritz 1957, 9; Schultz 1964, 122–23; Siporin 1976). Yet evidence provided by Goldsmith and Zeitlin (undated) and by Kinston and Rosser (1974) indicates that such sensitivity is difficult to sustain, that it may be replaced in relatively short order by feelings of hostility and prejudice, and that it can also diminish markedly as one moves from the center to the social and spatial periphery of the incident. One of the more compelling examples of this particular form of conceptual fragmentation can be found at Hiroshima. Lifton (1967) tells us that surviving victims of the 1954 atomic attack, although eligible for nominal government benefits, have been the objects of social and business discrimination. Conversely, those who actually died in this holocaust have been considered martyrs.

Another factor discouraging crisis intervention is the uneasy, even antagonistic, relationship that almost routinely develops between members of the various groups providing aid to survivors of a calamity. As I have written elsewhere, this disquiet can quickly turn into open animosity in the absence of good coordination of activities. Directors of relief and recovery operations for public service agencies, who are themselves under great stress and living with the constant threat of criticism from many quarters, can become extremely proprietary with respect to a specific catastrophe, and they usually resent outside specialists who—with unclear motives and beyond the control of organizational regulations—arrive on the scene to offer assistance (Greenamyre 1980, 22). Their reflected attitude seems to say, "This is my disaster. Go find one of your own."

Neither must it be assumed that those with expertise in the mental health disciplines are necessarily more likely than medical professionals to rush to the scene of every major emergency. They traditionally deal with individuals or small groups who seek them out (rather than the reverse), so they are possessed of the normal human suspicions concerning open-ended and unfamiliar situations. They are thus as reluctant as most people to initiate off-the-cuff and idiosyncratic activities that might promote misunderstanding, disagreement, or legal complications. Further, they are inclined to make the reasonable assumption that any support needed within their field of clinical competence has been anticipated and is provided for in existing contingency directives. These are the principal reasons why clearly written, unambiguous, and comprehensive disaster plans that assign resources adequate to meet the full range of human service needs are critical to the success of any relief and recovery program.

The third element in the problem of crisis intervention relates to those for whom the care is intended. It is this segment that is perhaps the most complicated. We have suggested that there is a strong tendency for disaster victims to reject therapy because it raises the specter of mental illness to both the recipients and those with whom they associate. In a society that places such a premium on the quality of self-reliance, however inappropriate and misguided excessive attachment to this attitude may sometimes prove to be, the internal conflict over whether or not to seek counsel can become particularly acute (Hsu 1961; Wolfenstein 1957). Consequently, programs that depend upon individuals to take the initiative when they need treatment have met with only marginal success. Another pervasive characteristic of our culture that disrupts the flow of care is that those belonging to a minority group do not always find emergency services readily accessible. As Kastenbaum (1974, 66–67) states in his Law of Inverse Magnitude, ethnic, age, and geographic biases may block the equitable distribution of critical forms of assistance. Moreover, members of some ethnic minorities and the lower socioeconomic classes, often the most vulnerable to the effects of a calamity, tend to avoid establishment representatives whenever alternative sources of information or support, however unreliable, appear to be available. This may be an irritant to those in charge of disaster operations, but it does not relieve them of the responsibility to ensure that all people within the community are adequately protected.

It seems appropriate to conclude with a consideration of how the character of future disasters will be influenced by interaction between human beings, their natural environments, and the increasingly synthetic ones they create. Hoebel (1972, 112) has called attention to the synergistic effects of both genetic and ecological instability on the development of all organisms. We are perhaps too quick to accept the accuracy of this particular insight without giving adequate thought to its more subtle implications.

Evidence continues to mount that it is unwise to view either our chromosomes or our physical surroundings as isolated elements in the human survival equation. Cultural activities, particularly those of technically advanced societies, have contributed to both an accelerating rate of genetic mutation and, invariably, a significant and generally detrimental modification of the habitat. This fact leads to the inevitable conclusion that technical, ecological, and demographic factors will continue to combine in ways that will alter the form as well as the magnitude of hazards faced by human populations. Yet it is necessary to remind ourselves that we are not dealing with a new order of collective behavior somehow rooted in the Industrial Revolution or, as White (1969) and others have hypothesized, in a peculiarly Western religious orientation. The march toward progress, with all of its possible pitfalls, can be traced directly back to the Stone Age hunters, miners, horticulturalists, hybrid stock breeders, and incipient engineers who were resolute in their attempts to gain greater control over the environment and thereby increase its productivity.

It is a consensus of the modern scientific fraternity, one with which Kroeber (1917) would undoubtedly agree, that the "Big Breakthrough" is about as rare as the "Great Man" in modern technological development. Most technical advances rest upon incremental changes that involve addition, redesign, or miniaturization of particular structural components; minor and presumably beneficial modifications in the molecular constituency of chemical substances; adoption of alternative power sources; achievement of greater manufacturing precision, or fabrication of seemingly more suitable construction materials. It may well be this almost nonchalant element in human progress, motivated by a need to solve immediate and obvious problems, that leads us, as Firey (1967) has observed, to be more concerned with the visible present than with a remote and ill-defined future for which dire and sometimes conflicting scenarios are offered. Global nuclear war, major new glaciations, melting polar ice caps, persistent chemically induced toxicity within all segments of the ecosystem, and widespread epidemics spawned by newly created and virulent microorganisms are but a few of the ominous possibilities for which debatable but scientifically credible cases have been made. When certain analysts who anticipate rampant population growth and misuse of an ever-diminishing resource base examine the social implications of current developmental trends in industrialized societies, projections can be equally grim (Meadows et al. 1972; Ophuls 1974).

Uncertainty over the precise nature of the most likely ultimate threats to a tolerable human existence also requires those persons responsible for emergency preparedness to focus upon manifest contemporary dangers rather than to become burdened by excessive fatalism over less verifiable ones beyond the horizon. They typically act on the optimistic and even admirable assumption that any crisis threatening the community can be contained and its effects mitigated through prompt application of thoughtful and technically correct recovery measures.

The state of Tennessee, historically a predominantly agricultural region that is now the scene of continuing industrial expansion, furnishes a reasonably representative locale for examining the foreseeable types of civil disasters. Accumulating seismic data indicate that severe earthquakes are a serious threat in a state whose geological foundations reveal abundant evidence of all four principal types of stress breaks, or faults. The power of physical forces being considered can perhaps be more clearly apprehended when it is realized that the land surface underlying Knoxville was once located in an adjacent county fifteen miles to the southeast (Luther 1977, 64–66). And the New Madrid earthquake of December 1811, emanating from an epicenter in southern Missouri, generated gigantic shock waves that continued until February 1812 and were felt as far away as Boston. The accompanying violent earth tremors terrified settlers for hundreds of miles and resulted in a massive alteration of the western Tennessee landscape. Yet this cataclysm, which is estimated to have reached or exceeded 7.6 on the Richter scale, produced remarkably few casualties because it occurred in an area with no large population concentrations. Should this level of seismic activity along the New Madrid fault be repeated—a possibility supported by a growing amount of information on hand at the Tennessee Emergency Management Agency—it could produce great loss of both life and property in such heavily developed urban areas as Memphis and in the many smaller communities now situated throughout the state's rugged and formerly sparsely settled interior. The presence of nuclear power facilities within the possible radius of terrestrial disturbance is an additional cause for concern.

Weather, too, continues to be a potentially destructive danger to Tennessee citizens, one made even more menacing by the present combination of increasing population density and modern technology. The state ranks among the top six in annual precipitation, and many seemingly capricious climatic changes can be traced to its position on the boundary between a humid continental zone on the north and equally humid subtropical conditions to the south. Tennessee is also in the grip of two peripheral and diverging paths of serious seasonal turbulence:

tornadoes and floods are ever-present environmental threats. Again, these traditional hazards are made more sinister by the presence of such modern cultural constants as uncoordinated channelization projects, injudicious floodplain development, and inadequate placement and supervision of toxic waste storage sites.

Cultural rather than environmental elements will without doubt play the major role in some of the catastrophes with which Tennessee residents, even those in relatively remote areas, will be called upon to deal. This fact was illustrated by an incident that took place on February 24, 1978, when the downtown section of the small west Tennessee community of Waverly was decimated by the explosion of 20,000 gallons of liquid propane leaking from a derailed railroad tank car. The blast and resulting inferno, in addition to producing considerable structural damage, left twelve persons dead and sent forty others to hospitals and burn centers throughout the region. Even in cases like this one, however, nature will contine to play a part, since wind direction and velocity, the character of the adjacent topography, and possible temperature inversions can often exert a critical influence on the course of events.

In summary, psychological trauma is an inevitable and deleterious companion to disaster. In each situation of this type, anxiety beyond the capacity of many persons to neutralize is consistently present. Moreover, such trauma is the product of an evolutionary process that begins with initial perception of the threat and continues to build through the impact stage. Even the cessation of physical injury and destruction does not put an end to the stress sequence. Not only do the psychic pressures continue to increase during the aftermath phase, but the circle of anxiety spreads to members of the community who may not have been directly threatened by the incident itself. Thus, trauma is an evolutionary phenomenon in both the individual and the collective sense.

These facts must be recognized if we are to avoid the mistaken presumption that certain disasters are somehow psychically traumatic while others are not. The potentially catastrophic situations to be faced by population centers in the future can be expected to have many features in common with those that have taxed the human will of societies since prehistoric times. It is mainly the hazardous technological specifics attending such incidents and the complexity of the societies themselves that will continue to change and, if the past is any guide, grow more imposing. Consequently, it becomes increasingly essential for any emergency management plan that seeks to restore members of a damaged community to their former levels of physical and mental self-sufficiency to contain adequate provisions for prompt and effective crisis intervention.

The Burden of Literacy in Native Languages as a Mark of Being Civilized

MARSHALL DURBIN

Linguists have a well-deserved reputation for fine and detailed analyses of small segments of data. This reputation is one they cherish and usually adhere to. I will depart from that tradition by attempting a much larger task. Here I want to demonstrate that one aspect of civilization—namely, writing—has a burdensome as well as an enlightening side.

THE LITERACY BURDEN IN CONTEMPORARY MESOAMERICA

During the years 1979 and 1980, I had the good fortune and privilege to work for the Mexican government as the linguistics director of an ethnolinguistics project. The goal of the project was to train Native Americans from seven indigenous language groups to be their own linguists. As many as ten students each from Yucatec Maya, Nahuatl, Mixtec, Otomi, Purepecha, Totonac, and Zapotec were selected from the approximately 26,000 bilingual teachers in Mexico. Criteria for entry into the program were that the students speak the native language fluently (and were so tested in interviews), have a close social and economic alliance to their home communities, and possess a high school diploma or its equivalent. The students were also interviewed about loyalty to their language, attitudes toward their own people, attitudes toward the hispanicization of Mexico, and the nature of their ultimate goals. For sixty-odd positions there were over 600 applications, and nearly 300 applicants were interviewed. Ability to write in the native language was not required, and hardly any applicant could do so. They were to be trained in social and cultural anthropology, ethnohistory, and linguistics, with the majority of the classroom, workshop, and field time being spent on linguistics. The training took place from June 1979 until May 1982, five days a week (except for major holidays), eight hours a day—each day being equally divided between classroom and workshop. Twice a year, approximately one and a half months were spent in fieldwork and library research. Sixty-two of these students received a bachelor's degree in ethnolinguistics and graduated in a ceremony in May 1982 in the presence of the President of the Republic.

The specific goal of the program was to train linguists who were native speakers of the indigenous languages of Mexico. In addition, the graduates were to achieve an understanding of their tribal and community history, not only since hispanicization but in pre-Columbian times as well, and they were to gain training in the social sciences—which, in reality, included more sociology and economics than social and cultural anthropology. The graduates would ideally become persons who could formulate native-language literacy programs in their home communities, initiate newspapers and radio broadcasts in the native language, and work on state and federal education projects aimed at indigenous speakers. In many cases the students were to return to their former teaching positions and initiate programs in their local schools. Overall, the aim was to strengthen and revitalize language loyalty for native indigenous languages.

Spatial constraints prohibit discussing the political problems—local, state, and federal—that cropped up; the ideological confrontation with the modern world; the students' lack of prior training; the dissension within the program as to its goals; the enmities—both old and new—that flared up among groups; and the overriding presence of as many as six foreign linguists. Rather, let me focus on one particular concern encountered in our day-to-day teaching.

One of the first goals of the program was to guide each student toward the development of an orthography for and literacy in his or her native language. Overall, the results were excellent: all the students did become literate in their native languages, and also arrived at an understanding of orthographical and literacy problems in general.

The status of the native language in relation to Spanish plagued us, however, in some cases leaving questions unresolved even at the end of the program. There were three particular problems:

(1) The belief that the native language is inferior to Spanish and to such other European languages as English and French.
(2) A belief that writing in the native language must incorporate aspects of Spanish orthography.
(3) A belief that writing in the native language is for novelty, ornamentation, and recording ordinary speech, but not for discourse, emotional expression, abstractions, or instructional matters.

Although they are obviously related, I will discuss each of these problems separately.

The native language is inferior to Spanish and other European languages. Though the students were selected for loyalty to both their native language and their home communities, it became evident that many felt their language to be inferior in structure and for expression in the modern world. Within a year's time we were able to overcome this belief through continual comparison of each native language structure with Spanish (and occasionally with other European languages). The morning classroom lectures (in Spanish) on linguistic structures presented aspects of Spanish structure: the phonemes, their allophones, the complementarity or free variation of phonemic distribution. The same concepts were applied to the native languages in the afternoon workshops. In sum, we were constantly forming contrastive grammars of Spanish and the native languages.

Ironically, we were not initially aware that our students suffered from the "language inferiority complex" and that we were correcting the problem by means of contrastive grammars. Only after a year did we learn of it, when the students informed us that they had originally regarded their languages as inferior to Spanish, that they were old-fashioned, and that they had been ashamed to speak them among other younger people. Several students reported that more people now spoke the language more often in their home communities. Of course, what had actually happened was that the students themselves spoke their language more often and with more speakers, once their embarrassment and shame had been replaced with pride and confidence in their native tongue. In fact, they were now using the language in more contexts than ever before. In summary, the "language inferiority complex" was overcome by teaching detailed comparative structures.

Writing in the native language must incorporate aspects of Spanish orthography. Many of our students were descendants of people who had developed indigenous writing systems that for the most part were in use until nearly 1600. But the hispanicization process, with considerable duress and pain, literally eliminated the native orthography and imposed a Latinate orthography, in which the native languages continued to be written. The imposition of the Latin alphabet and the presumed superiority of Spanish had been so successful that many of our students were unhappy to learn that certain letters—*f, d, g,* etc.—need not be used in their native orthographies, and they expressed considerable resistance to the idea that *š* and *č* might be represented by means different from the conventional Spanish *x* and *ch*. Also, there was reluctance to accept the marking of tone in the four tonal languages in the group. We overcame these difficulties by demonstrating that writing is not the language but a separate system, which can show solidarity with or manifest independence from the national culture. After about one year each group chose an orthography based largely on social, practical, and political considerations rather than its relation to the Spanish orthography.

Writing in the native language is for novelty, ornamentation, and recording speech but not for discourse, emotional expression, abstractions, or instructional matters. Regrettably, we were not able to resolve this particular issue. I was considerably disappointed when only a handful of students (e.g., one out of ten Mayans) chose to write and defend their bachelors' theses in the native language—even though bilingual secretaries were available with appropriately keyed typewriters, bilingual readers and examiners were present, and all the students were now literate and had even been trained in the colonial paleography of their respective languages. Although there were many excellent theses on phonology, morphology, dialect studies, orthography formation, and the interpretation of native post-Columbian documents, the use of the written native language was mostly restricted to ornamentation in a dedicatory quote or message, an introduction, or a preface, or to the occasional word sprinkled here and there. Furthermore, those who did write their theses in the native language were not able to achieve a style above that of colloquial speech, often employing rapid contractions comparable to the English "Jeet?" for "Did you eat?" They had not realized that written words could be manipulated and restructured in their presentation and that the written word could determine the presentation of ideas in a manner very different from that of the spoken word. This was not the case with Spanish. Utilizing literary and scholarly styles, some students achieved eloquence in written Spanish; in their own languages, however, they had no style apart from that of colloquial speech. These remarks are not in criticism of the students. Neither the instructors nor the students had sufficient time in those three short years to confront this issue adequately. I remain uncertain as to how to proceed in correcting the problem. Nor is the situation by any means unique to Mesoamerica. Our own ancestors apparently experienced the same burden of being literate in their native language.

THE LITERACY BURDEN IN ANGLO-SAXON EUROPE

The history of Germanic and consequently of English orthography is intimately tied to the history of a Latin-based alphabet. The runes of northern Europe were written in a language that was neither Old Norse, Proto-Scandinavian, nor Primitive Germanic. Rather, these runes (which are found from southern Scandinavia to as far south as Hungary and Rumania, and in Poland and part of the Ukraine) are generally thought to have been written in a protolanguage referred to as Northwest Germanic, which presumably is ancestral to the Germanic languages of Scandinavia, to modern-day German, and to the Lowland Germanic languages of English, Frisian, and Dutch. The first known inscriptions appeared in about A.D. 200 on hand objects such as spears. In the fifth century, they occurred on more permanent objects such as stone stelae, but by the sixth century their popularity had begun to decline.

During the sixth century, runic inscriptions were engraved on gold imitations of Roman medallions. In England they survived for some centuries as a learned pastime appearing on crosses, boxes, and other personal objects. The language they expressed was never elevating, consisting mostly of personal names or short sentences such as "I, Klewagasti, the son of Holti, made this horn." The inscriptions were rarely longer than forty words (one notable exception being the Ruthwell Cross, with eighty-five words), and in several instances they contain single words repeated to form, apparently, a magical chant. In some cases, the inscriptions make no sense at all. In sum, rune-writing served as a pastime, a form of ornamentation for the uneducated. As Haugen (1976, 23) notes, "Rune-writing never achieved the recognition of regular scribal use on parchment in more than a thousand years of use." He further suggests that runes were in all probability an attempt to initiate a writing system for the Germanic languages, but that function was ultimately assumed by the Latin alphabet.

There appears to be nothing inherently complicated about the runes that would prevent their use for scribal practices. They are roughly modeled upon Latin (perhaps to some extent on Greek) with each letter having a name, which made them easily learned as a system. Rather than fault the runic system, I would suggest that the users of the runes were probably suffering from the same beliefs about language superiority and inferiority that I observed among my students in Mexico. In this case, the Germanic scribes apparently believed that the Latin alphabet and language were to be used for abstract concepts, while the "native" runes were appropriate only for ornamentation.

This hypothesis is borne out by examining the introduction of the Anglo-Saxons to Latin. The Anglo-Saxons entered the British Isles by invitation between A.D. 446 and 454, and then later took the southern half of the main island by conquest. They were no doubt immediately brought into contact with the Latin language and written Latin, since the Romans had been in the isles for over 500 years, and many Celtic speakers were also proficient in both speaking and writing Latin. There is no evidence of Celtic writing in a Latin script from that period, though as early as A.D. 430 in Ireland we find the use of a variant of the runic thorn (ð) in St. Patrick's charter granting indulgences to benefactors of Clastonbury. Many Anglo-Saxons, too, must have become relatively fluent and literate in Latin in the period following A.D. 450; philologists have noted the introduction of several lexical items from Latin into Anglo-Saxon at this time. Also, Procopius, a Roman writer, produced a short history of England in Latin in 550, and in 547 a British monk named Gilda, a Celt, wrote a tract on the miseries of Britain. While Anglo-Saxons were undoubtedly writing Latin during this period, it is not until A.D. 604, shortly after their acceptance of Christianity, that we encounter the first evidence of written Anglo-

Saxon. It appears in a grant by Æthelberht, King of Kent, to St. Andrew's, Rochester, of land at Southgate on April 28, 604. The text consists of seventeen words that form a property description:

> Fram suðgeate west andlanges wealles oð norðlanan to stræte; & swa east fram stræte oð doddinghyrnan ongean bradgeat.

This translates: "From the southgate west along the wall and then in a northerly line to the street. Then east from the street and on to the corner opposite the gate."

Carlton (1970) has noted that these early land boundary descriptions in Anglo-Saxon can be described as a series of prepositional phrases. They never exceed 175 words, and they are usually preceded by several paragraphs in Latin describing the conditions of the charter and followed by a closing Latin paragraph with signatures and titles in Latin.

Not until A.D. 680 do we find a complete letter in Anglo-Saxon: a translation of a Latin letter from Pope Agatha to Athered, King of the Mercains, and to Theodore, Archbishop, granting privileges to the monastery of Petersborough. This letter and others that followed were in all probability heavily influenced by Latin in their style and syntax. Only with the beginning of the ninth century do we encounter written Anglo-Saxon that is neither a translation from Latin nor a property boundary statement. During the ninth, tenth, and eleventh centuries, Anglo-Saxon writing bloomed in heroic poetry, especially during Alfred's time, when Latin fell into disuse. The Anglo-Saxons had finally solved their language inferiority problem, at least partially. The failure to write in the native language for nearly 350 years, however, provides evidence again that it was felt not to be a proper medium for poetry, heroic deeds, history, emotional expression, or abstractions. Rather, the written native language was used for ornamentation or, at most, to express practical and colloquial speech. Concomitantly, there was quite probably the belief that the native language orthography must incorporate as many aspects of the superior language orthography as possible: thus the failure and eventual abandonment of the runic system. An overall conclusion, then, is that the Anglo-Saxons, though not conquered by a Latin-speaking people, took the same psychological stance with regard to the relationship between their own language and a "superior" language as did my students in Mexico.

CONCLUSION

In what might be called "psycho-archaeology," I have used data from a modern group and compared them with data from a historical group, the nature of the data being patterns of literacy acquisition in the native language. Where the two patterns have coincided, I have extrapolated from one psychological set to the other, thus making inferences about Anglo-Saxon thought patterns that I could do in no other way. Perhaps there are errors in the data, but I do not believe there are errors in the reasoning process.

Some might say that the conclusions are uninteresting, since all native writing systems take time for acceptance. But this is not always the case. We have no similar evidence in the adoption of the Sanskrit writing system. Even better examples are the Cyrillic and Cherokee writing systems, which are modified forms of the Greek and English systems, respectively; they were used immediately for all forms of communication and have not languished as cultural ornaments. I believe my reasoning is sound because I have used the comparative method, so beloved of linguists. I have always wondered why archaeologists do not employ the comparative method with its system of correspondence sets and cognates. Doing so might allow archaeologists to reconstruct protohouses in the same manner that linguists have reconstructed Indo-European; it might also allow them to move from an exclusive interest in material culture to an exploration of the psychological aspects of prehistoric society.

As seen in the Native American and Anglo-Saxon cases, writing can be a burden of civilization. At times, it prevents us from expressing the best of our thought in our own native language. Yet we must not forget that writing is also a device that moves us away from the false starts, the hesitations, the psychological interruptions, and the practicality of everyday speech. With writing, we can enter into a more abstract, more emotional, more heroic, and even more human world than that afforded to us by the oral medium.

Celistino and His Discontents: A Metalogue with Civilization and Its Discontents

GREGORY G. RECK

INTRODUCTION

> Anthropology, abstractly conceived as the study of man, is actually the study of men in crisis by men in crisis. (Diamond 1974, 93)

Since the beginning of our discipline, anthropologists have made a living of sorts from the discontents that civilization has wrought upon indigenous peoples around the world. Engaged in a kind of "salvage anthropology" that recorded band and tribal cultures even while they were being destroyed, anthropologists carved out their academic niche as the champions of disappearing peoples. Armed with the mighty sword of cultural relativism, we fought the war with civilization in the ivy-covered halls of academe. Small battles were won, but the direction of the destruction was not altered. The advent of applied anthroplogy since World War II is, in a sense, the formal recognition of this fact. The problems to which we apply our knowledge and skills are precisely those resulting from our failure to stem the spread of contemporary imperial civilization. Less than thirty years ago, Lévi-Strauss (1955) could write about a world on the wane; today we must, in large part, write about a world that no longer is.

Why has so little changed despite the best intentions of most anthropologists? We have searched for the answer to this question in the world economic and political system, in the growth of technology, and in the insatiable culture of consumption, all of which are undoubtedly significant areas to be considered. But we have failed in large part to search within ourselves, to come fully to grips with the paradox of our situation. Our general perception of the issue has been one-sided: we have attempted to understand the impact of civilization on those whom we study, but we have failed to examine seriously what civilization has done to provide us with that reified identity that we so dearly cherish—the anthropologist.

In reality, we, like the people we study, are victims of civilization. The discontents of civilization are to be found as much in what we do as anthropologists as in the lives of those whom we study. The power that we perceive ourselves to possess is largely an illusion, resulting from our acceptance of the historical myth of the Enlightenment and the subsequent scientific revolution as a process of total intellectual liberation, rather than the limited liberation that it was. In reality, the civilization that gave rise to anthropology and continues to support its existence is at the very same time engaged in crippling its potential. A failure to recognize this paradox is a symptom of the successful debilitation of our field.

This crippling is in part a consequence of what Gouldner (1970, 495) has called "methodological dualism," an ideology that focuses on the qualitative differences between the social scientist and those whom he or she observes. Demanding a separation of researcher and object, this ideology views their contact with suspicion and fear, as a contamination of the research system. This fear is not so much anchored in a positive pursuit of truth, however, as it is in the negative avoidance of oneself. With this ideology we do not have to confront our living passions—the hope, fear, joy, and anger of existence—for we constantly have our research design by our side, making disembodied sense out of what we experience.

The paradox, as Diamond has pointed out (1974, 93), is that both the anthropologist and those studied, despite opposing positions in the research equation, are objects of contemporary imperial civilization. We who have been reduced to objects by civilization have in turn sought to flee our alienation by transforming those who live on the margins of civilization into our own image. The chasm only widens. For by objectifying others, we succeed only in further objectifying ourselves. Rather than confronting our situation, we have chosen to create a profession out of our alienation. In so doing, we have remained consistent with the consequences of contemporary civilization: to make thought abstract, to objectify self and others, and to reduce the world to an efficient equation.

The objectification of self and others in anthropology and other social sciences has both a political and a personal dimension. Politically, it maintains a nonpartisan self-image that inhibits consideration of the critical struggles in the world today and provides contemporary civilization with the assurance of the benign nature of our discipline. In this sense, the modern concept of objectivity is anchored in the nineteenth century's European scientific societies, which promised governments that they would not become involved in matters of church or state (Arendt 1969, 271). Objectivity is consistent with the utilitarianism of contemporary civilization in which everything, humans included, is valued according to its use (Gouldner 1970, 102). Nonutilitarian attachments to objects—transforming them into subjects—are seen as impeding "rational" exchange. Since humans in contemporary civilization are viewed essentially as commodities, reducing them to objects is consistent with the need to buy, sell, and use them and ourselves. The objectification of self and others in anthropology has helped to ensure the security of the self-fulfilling prophecy of civilization that the human is an object. In this sense, objectivity is alienation from self and others and has its origin in the anomie of the nineteenth century (Gouldner 1970, 103).

Our paradox cannot be resolved; it can only be confronted through a reflexive anthropology that holds dialogue between analysis, self, and other. We must confront our situation not only through our work but through our lives; not only in what we do but also in who we are. If authentic, this confrontation will produce an unrelenting critical perspective that fights the reduction of ourselves and others into objects.

THE METALOGUE: ANALYSIS, SELF, AND OTHER

> A metalogue is a conversation . . . [in which] not only do the participants discuss the problem but the structure of the conversation as a whole is also relevant to the same subject. (Bateson 1972, 1)

Analysis. The village of Jonotla is located approximately 100 miles east-northeast of Mexico City in the *Sierra Norte* of the state of Puebla. Jonotla is the center of the *municipio* and has a population of approximately 1,500 individuals living in some 300 households. The village is inhabited by both *mestizos* and Nahuatl-speaking Indians who possess cultural differences and distinct ethnic identities much like those described for Mesoamerica by other anthropologists (de la Fuente 1967; Gillin 1945; Madsen and Madsen 1974; Wagley 1965).

According to recently collected local oral history and an early Spanish document (Rayón 1581), Jonotla was founded in the twelfth century A.D. by Chichimec peoples who had migrated southward from northern Mexico. They moved into an area already inhabited by Totonac peoples tied to the ceremonial center at El Tajin, located some fifty miles to the northeast. During the fifteenth century, the Aztecs from Tenochtitlan established hegemony over the region and the village. Today, the village is located in an area of both Nahuatl- and Totonaco-speaking Indians, a reminder of its pre-Spanish experience with diverse peoples.

While the Aztec civilization subjugated local peoples through forced payment of tribute and sacrificial victims, the Spanish who followed in the sixteenth century managed to politically and economically harness the lives of Jonotecans more completely. The founding of the nation of Mexico in the nineteenth century continued the process of subjugating the Indians of Jonotla to expanding imperial civilizations. Thus, the village of Jonotla has been constructed out of successive layers of control and domination by archaic, feudal, and contemporary civilizations during the prehistoric, colonial, and postcolonial periods.

In this sense, the changes that have taken place over the past several decades are in large measure a continuation of a process that began hundreds of years ago. Nevertheless, the current changes in Jonotla are part of the final assault on the barriers that Indian communities have traditionally established against the various civilizations of which they have less than willingly been a part. These barriers created what Wolf (1955; 1957) has called closed corporate communities. In Mexico, as in most other Latin American countries, closed corporate communities are rapidly disappearing as capitalist production and government "development" programs penetrate the socioeconomic conditions that once enabled Indian communities to retain a modicum of control over themselves and their identity.

Central to the maintenance of these barriers is an economic system oriented toward subsistence production, as opposed to the market, and a strong civil-religious hierarchy that wields a degree of internal control over economic production and distribution and political authority. For centuries, Indian communities have been faced with the difficult and conflicting tasks of wresting a living from often less than hospitable lands, meeting the demands of the larger political-economic system of which they are dependent satellites, and preserving a sense of community control, meaning, and identity. Many, like Jonotla, had managed to do so—with varying degrees of success—because of their ability to maintain noncapitalist social and economic forms. However, in Jonotla and elsewhere in Mexico (e.g., Greenberg 1981), the full penetration of capitalist economic forms has successfully undermined subsistence production, the civil-religious hierarchy, and the associated ideology of egalitarianism and community participation.

Self-Reflection. In other words, the village of Jonotla was ripe for a North American anthropologist who had an interest in the abstract issues of socioeconomic change. It got one.

Born in Hidalgo County in the Rio Grande Valley of south Texas and reared in a liberal, working-class family in a Houston neighborhood where the Mexican-American community nearby suffered the indignity of having its public school named Alamo Elementary, I was made for anthropology in Mexico. When I had my inevitable conversion experience to anthropology as a confused third-year sociology major, I knew immediately that I would do my fieldwork in Mexico. I somehow finished my graduate studies while participating in the social and political protest movements of the late 1960s in Washington, D.C., sandwiching between them considerable anthropology, some Allen Ginsberg, Sartre, Nietszche, and the Rolling Stones. And then suddenly I was off to Mexico to do *real* anthropology. It all seemed so magnificently natural.

I jumped right into my research with an implicit conviction that Jonotla was, indeed, to be my village. After nearly three months of research, I had completed a household census, engaged in hundreds of formal and informal interviews, participated in formal and informal social interaction, and started to abstract patterns that seemed important to my research focus on socioeconomic change. The stacks of cards and papers on my small desk were starting to look impressive. I was feeling very much the professional anthropologist with a growing pile of reasonable data and even a few interesting experiences to share with future colleagues as we sat around the bar telling field stories at the next convention. I was filled with anticipation for the future.

One thing I had not anticipated was meeting Celistino de la Cruz. Our initial meeting was not very memorable: he showed my wife and me around the upstairs rooms of a house in which we subsequently rented two rooms. He and his wife and four-year-old daughter lived downstairs in the same house.

At first I saw him as an ideal informant. Born into a Nahuatl-speaking Indian family from a nearby village, he had moved as a young boy with his family to Jonotla. His father had come "to look for centavos," as Celistino put it, after being kicked off the land he had sharecropped for some fifteen years. This, and a series of additional familial tragedies, had cut Celistino loose from his past, leaving him in a sometimes desperate, sometimes almost whimsical, search for his place in a changing world. As I talked with him more and more, I found him the best example of the patterns I was abstracting from my data: an Indian who, through a series of life events related to the larger process of socioeconomic change in the region, was severed from his Indian past and pushed hesitatingly toward a new cultural identity. I was collecting other examples and case studies, but there was something different about Celistino. I sensed it at the time, but I decided to worry about it later.

The Other. Not surprisingly, it was raining again. Although Jonotla experienced a rainy and a dry season, the latter was not as dry as in most other areas of central Mexico. These rugged mountains, which vividly revealed both the ravages and the beauty of old age, captured the moisture moving inland from the Gulf of Mexico, enabling the region to support a luxurious green mantle throughout the year. For Jonotecans, however, rain at the height of the coffee-picking season meant no work for the day. For those like Celistino, who owned no land and depended upon the wage labor of the relatively short coffee season for the bulk of their yearly income, the rain was not welcome.

Celistino finished his morning meal with his family and walked into a small vacant room on the east end of the house. Only weeks before, the room had been occupied by a young medical student who had spent a mandatory year providing sporadic health care for the village. The young doctor had been less than enthusiastic about his task, spending at least as much time back home in the city of Puebla as he did in Jonotla. He often said that the people of Jonotla made themselves sick through their ignorance, and there was, therefore, little that he could do.

Despite this attitude, or perhaps because of it, Celistino had developed a sort of admiration for the young doctor. He seemed to be from a world that Celistino imagined he could be a part of if only he could discover the key to participation. It was for this reason that Celistino had spent many an enjoyable hour probing the doctor's knowledge. Now, all that was left in the room was a single chair and a box of discarded medicine, an old pharmaceutical encyclopedia, a pregnancy calendar, and a dictionary. These constituted the legacy of a man who was successful in terms of a world that Celistino was struggling to comprehend.

He took out a small spiral notebook from the box and started to write in it. It was a book of notes to himself, mostly about his future. For someone engaged in a daily struggle to feed himself and his family, it was an unusual activity. But somehow the magical world of words was symbolic of that imaginary world, much like the world of the young doctor, that Celistino had created from the memories of his broken past and the hopes of an insecure future.

The book was a refuge from the frustrations he encountered almost daily. Once recorded, his plans and observations about the future seemed to take on a reality that they could never have outside the confines of the written page: the store he would own, the land he would buy, the big financial deal he would make. Tomorrow he would be struggling to pick as many coffee beans as he could, but today important plans had to be made. Chances were excellent that none of them would be fulfilled. The attainable accomplishments of his Indian past were no longer available, and he had no viable access to the rewards that his new world dangled in front of him. Yet he spent the rainy days writing dreams in his brown spiral notebook.

Analysis. The penetration of new economic forms into the village was the result of internal and external factors that complemented one another. On the one hand, internal factors such as population growth, a decrease in the productivity of the land, and inheritance patterns that resulted in smaller land holdings in each new generation were producing severe pressures on the economic base of *campesinos*. With approximately 6 percent of the households, mostly *mestizo*, holding over 60 percent of the land, and almost one-fourth of the households completely landless, internal economic pressures were very real. On the other hand, government projects such as the construction of the first road into the community in 1969, electricity in the early 1970s, and particularly the coffee production program constituted external pressures that promoted modification in economic production.

The previously closed nature of the community was giving way to an economic system that increasingly relied upon (1) coffee as a cash crop with the accompanying deterioration of subsistence agriculture, (2) plural wage employment and short-term *centavo* commerce, and (3) a significant out-migration of individuals seeking employment, particularly young people entering the work force for the first time. Taken together, these factors disrupted the community's ability to insulate itself from external control and inextricably melded it to the larger economic system. The result was a system increasingly operating according to certain basic market principles: economic interdependency; production for the market; transactions based on market forces; household emphasis on maximizing profit; extension of personal as well as community contacts; and some dependency upon national and international economic forces.

Self-Reflection. Just at the time that I should have been feeling good about my research, my life became shaky. I had been well prepared to experience and handle what my profession referred to as "culture shock," but what I was experiencing seemed not to fit that shopworn idea. Certainly, the stress was present, but rather than attempting to draw upon the strengths of my personality and training to withstand the pressures, I found myself surrendering to them. It was all a bit frightening, not because I feared that I would fail in my fieldwork, but rather because I didn't know what sort of person might emerge from the long tunnel that I was entering.

Things would have been easier had I been facing only research problems. I had always felt that a major difference between anthropological field research and the research of most other social scientists was that the others confronted *research* problems while anthropologists confronted *real* problems. Now, I knew that it was true. My research, my self, and my life were headed for a change that I could not foresee.

At this point, two experiences provided some intangible sense of direction to what had been vaguely but painfully churning in my mind. They happened during the same week in November.

I had stopped to speak to an old blind Indian named Don Chalo. Leading me up into the small chapel outside of which he made his living by selling herbs and religious articles, he asked me to describe what I saw. After what I thought was a reasonably complete description of the chapel, Don Chalo mildly chastised me for limiting my description to, as he put it, "things outside of the soul"—the objective world. At another time in my life—or in my research—I might have brushed his dissatisfaction aside. At this particular point, however, his comments seemed to thrust deeply into the very heart of what I was doing in the village—transforming passionate life into lifeless data.

A few days later, I returned home from a morning of conversations and stopped to talk with Celistino, who was standing in front of our house. We were approached by a young man who had quite a reputation as a *macho*. He was very drunk, and it was not long before he tried to engage me in a verbal duel over our respective masculine attributes, ranging from various anatomical features to the virtues of our wives and mothers, and finally, to the durability of our wristwatches when smashed against the cobblestoned street.

My initial thoughts were only of how I might extricate myself from this unwanted situation. I would have welcomed the opportunity to *observe* such a verbal duel, but personal involvement was quite another thing. I had neither desire nor need, I thought, to exchange subtle insults with a man I hardly knew. My meager responses to the verbal jabs reflected my lack of enthusiasm.

Slowly this all changed. At some point—I cannot remember precisely when—I began to take the encounter seriously. Alternately threatened, proud, angered, and afraid, I had entered some unknown place within me. I was no longer collecting data or even having an anthropologically relevant experience. My research design was nowhere to be seen. The wall constructed out of the roles of anthropologist and informant, cemented together by the objectification of self and other, had momentarily crumbled. There was no object of study, no professional who studied and layman who was studied. I could not hide and pretend there was no one here but an anthropologist.

When the encounter finally ended an hour later, I stumbled exhausted and weak-kneed to my room and tried to record what had happened. I had difficulty recalling many details. Overwhelmed by feelings of embarrassment, astonishment, and guilt, I thought about seeking out my worthy opponent to apologize for what I had implied about his sister, and I worried about how this incident might affect my research. The wall had been repaired, and I had returned to my world.

The Other. Celistino awoke before the light of the new day spread shadows across the village. He had been hired to pick coffee in the fields of Andres Ortuno de Gaona, the wealthiest and most powerful person in the community. The day promised to be dry and warm, a fact that meant Celistino would be able to pick more coffee beans and thus earn more. Paid by the weight of the beans he picked, Celistino could earn as much as $1.50 for the day if he worked long, hard hours. Later, Señor Ortuno would be able to sell the beans picked by Celistino that day for between $25 and $30.

Celistino was fortunate, compared with many of his neighbors. He was healthy and strong, and he had a reputation as a hard worker. During the four- to five-month coffee-picking season, he had little trouble finding work. As a landless wage laborer, however, the remainder of the year was more difficult, so he counted heavily on the coffee season for the $200 or so needed to sustain his small family through the year.

The sun was nudging the darkness from the green mountains as Celistino set out on the thirty-minute walk to the coffee groves. It was at such quiet times that his hopes and dreams tumbled loosely through his mind. He would think of schemes that he was certain would make "the *centavos* fall" sufficiently for him to purchase what he imagined would be his independence: a small store.

Too quickly the voices of others who already had arrived at Señor Ortuno's coffee field brought Celistino's thoughts back to the day at hand. The men spent little time greeting each other; instead, they went right to work, nimbly stripping the branches of their bright red beans.

Celistino worked next to Silvano Zaragoza, a frail man who looked much older than his forty years. At first, they talked little; when they did, it was of the weather or the quality of the season's coffee harvest. But soon Silvano was coughing and complaining of feeling weak. Celistino suggested he go home, but Silvano continued to pick, mumbling about his family's need for every *centavo* they could find. Celistino said little, but he understood all too well. Silvano had a wife and four children. Like Celistino, he owned no land. But unlike Celistino, he was sickly, and thus wage labor was not as readily available to him. In their own ways, both were left with only one choice, as Celistino would say: "working in someone else's mud."

At lunchtime the men sat in the shade, eating, laughing, and talking. Celistino shared his fresh *tortillas* with Silvano, who had brought very little to eat. He took care that the others did not notice.

As the men were preparing to return to work after lunch, Señor Ortuno's oldest son, Rafael, approached on horseback. He greeted them all amicably and asked for an accounting of the amount of coffee each had picked. The amounts varied slightly from man to man, but the son seemed satisfied until he reached Silvano, who reported an amount only slightly less than the others. Rafael Ortuno stared and then smiled at Silvano. The men knew something was going to happen. Dismounting from his horse, the young man asked to see what the older man had picked. Silvano, his straw hat in his hands and his head bent toward the ground, turned and walked over to a large burlap bag. "These are mine," he said softly. Everyone could see that the bag contained considerably fewer kilos of beans than Silvano had reported. It had been a foolish thing for him to do, since an accurate weighing would be made at the end of the day.

Rafael Ortuno spit out a short and derisive laugh. "You are a fool," he said. "You have nothing without this work. Nothing. We give you this work out of the mercy of our souls. You are nothing without us. Don't come to work tomorrow." He turned away and led his horse down the narrow path toward the village.

The men returned to their work, but Silvano slumped to the ground. "Why did you lie, Silvano?" Celistino asked.

"I don't know," he replied softly. "I was afraid that I had not picked enough and that Señor Ortuno would not hire me again. I thought that I could pick faster in the afternoon so that they would not notice my lie."

The other men continued to pick. Celistino stood next to Silvano and looked silently at him. It was several moments before Celistino was able to return to work.

Analysis. The final assault on the minimal village defenses against exploitation has effectively severed the institutional support for the maintenance of an Indian identity. That identity is anchored in a system known as *el modo del indio,* the way of the Indian. It is a complex notion centered on corn cultivation as an economic, social, and religious activity. The basic goal is subsistence, with a secondary goal of capital accumulation directed at service to the saints and to the community. This service is sustained through an ideology of reciprocity and egalitarianism.

As cash crops and wage labor displace the traditional subsistence economy, the interwoven factors that constitute *el modo del indio* are dissected. An individual Indian can no longer interact with non-Indians as a representative of a distinct ethnic group. Instead, they meet as individuals representing individual interests. As has been demonstrated (e.g., Crumrine and Crumrine 1969; Greenberg 1981; Reck 1978), the loss of Indian identity occurs when internal and external social relations are individualized. For it is then that the previously external threats, which helped maintain a sense of unity, become internal threats as individual competes with individual.

Indians in Mexico have in the past survived total incorporation into contemporary civilization by refusing, as Eric Wolf (1959, 219) has written, to play a game that will always seek its first victims among their own neighbors. Postcolonial mechanisms of exploitation have now been replaced by capitalistic modes, and the Indians of Jonotla no longer have the means to stay out of the game.

This situation is particularly difficult for individuals like Celistino de la Cruz, who have been set adrift in a world that no longer plays by the old rules. Lacking an Indian community to return to, uncertain of whether they would return even if they could, they search for some new identity. The one offered to them by contemporary civilization is the same one offered to them throughout the historical past—to be the pariahs of the larger society. But they no longer have an Indian community to provide them with the hope that the judgment of the larger society does not really matter.

Self-Reflection. The stacks of note cards on my desk continued to grow; maps, census data, network charts, and other trinkets of my short life in Jonotla filled the corners of my work area. By this time I even had an extensive notebook on Celistino. Despite all of these quite proper anthropological curios, my commitments had shifted considerably.

I had arrived in Jonotla primarily to make some sort of contribution to an anthropological understanding of socioeconomic change in rural

Mexico. Whatever my traditional anthropological disclaimers, the people of Jonotla were but a means to that end. I had selected them, and although I didn't know specifically what they were going to give to me, I was confident that it would add up to what I wanted: a reasonably good anthropological study.

They had something different in mind, however. Celistino and others had neatly carved away the facade of anthropologist and informants to reveal the persons beneath. I had never been an abstraction to them, and they challenged my attempts to turn them into examples or case studies. As a consequence, my primary commitment had turned toward the struggle to understand and retain in my research and writing the lived passion of those who were sharing their lives with me.

I had come to understand that the idealized features of social science research—objectivity and detachment, power and control, precision and efficiency, bureaucracy and standardization—are reflections of our crisis as voyagers within contemporary civilization (German and Reck 1978). We choose to ignore that surge of life in ourselves and others, smothering it in a dense fog of terminology, tables, abstractions, and professionalism. Contemporary civilization has denied us our humanity, and in our search to regain what we have had taken from us, we have denied it to others.

I began to realize that the reason Celistino seemed different from the others was that he refused to remain an object of my analysis. This was not only because of his own unique personality but even more because of the relationship we had. It began as an instrumental relationship defined by my need for data, but through the relative absence of any instrumental motives on his part, it evolved into what he called *pura amistad,* pure friendship.

The understanding that resulted could not be stored in a card file or coded for a computer. It was an understanding linked inextricably to a relationship—as is all understanding, whether or not we choose to recognize it. It was based in my growing recognition of the depth of our kinship with those whom we try to study. In our different ways and worlds, Celistino and I shared a common struggle: as Richardson (1975) has characterized it, the impossible task of being human. In this sense, he was a human colleague, struggling with his own competencies to understand and thrive in his world, just as I was in mine. We were, in a real sense, the other side of each other.

The Other. Celistino sat at a small table in Don Vicente's store, drinking small shots of *aguardiente* and chasing it with Orange Crush. The room was filled with men who had spent the day working in someone else's mud. Most were gathered in small groups, but outside the doorway several men sat on the ground alone, drinking the solitude from their lives.

As Celistino casually chatted with his friends, Silvano Zaragoza entered the store, purchased a small shot glass of *aguardiente,* and went back through the doorway into the darkness. Celistino excused himself and made his way outside. As his eyes adjusted to the mountain night, he found Silvano slumped against the side of the store, his muddy legs stretched out in front of him.

Celistino approached slowly. "Good evening, Silvano. How are you?" he asked.

Silvano looked up as if startled to hear such a friendly voice. Smiling, he returned the greeting and patted the ground next to him. Celistino eased himself down. The two men said nothing for a moment.

"You haven't been picking coffee for Don Andres recently, Silvano," Celistino broke the silence. "Did that little turd Rafael talk to his father?"

Silvano finished the contents of his glass. "I went to Don Andres the next day, but he said he didn't need my labor just now. I told him how much I needed the money, but all he would say is maybe next week."

Celistino took Silvano's glass from his hand and went back into the store. Moments later he returned with two full glasses. Silvano continued: "This morning, Rafael came pounding on my door and asked me whether I wanted to earn some *centavos.* 'Of course,' I said. He smiled and patted me on the shoulder and told me to bring my strong back to the plaza." Silvano explained how he had spent the day carrying 100-pound sacks of coffee beans from Don Andres's store to the plaza, where they were loaded on a truck bound for the regional market in Zacapoaxtla.

Celistino looked at Silvano's small frame, not much more than 100 pounds itself, and wondered how he had managed to make it through the day.

"When the day was finished," Silvano continued, "Rafael gave me five pesos, fifteen *centavos* for each sack, and a 'gift' of twenty *centavos.* He said that I could work again tomorrow." He paused to finish the *aguardiente*. "I told him I was not a burro. He said that I was right—a burro is worth more."

Celistino said nothing. He knew what Silvano was feeling. He, too, struggled in a world where one had to earn his right to exist and where his worth was measured in terms of how many kilos of coffee beans he could pick or how many sacks of coffee beans he could carry. Indians had always been treated this way by the outside world; it had been the same for Celistino's father. But for Celistino's father, that world was not his total world. He lived a significant part of his life in a world where one's right to exist was a given, and where human worth was intrinsic to that existence. The fact that this stress on human equality was in part a reaction to the oppression and disenfranchisement of Indians by other classes in society mattered little. It was a refuge Celistino and Silvano no longer had.

Celistino put his face close to Silvano's and said, "This afternoon you may have been a burro, Silvano, but remember that tonight and tomorrow, when Andres and Rafael Ortuno are not using you, then you are a man." The two men stared at each other until broad grins spread across their faces like the light of the new morning. They laughed until they could laugh no more.

Modern Civilization and the Evolution of Personality: We Have Collapsed Infancy into Senility

Arden R. King

This title compels its author to set out a number of definitions and assumptions. I assume that it is intellectually more economical to maintain that all characteristic behavior is learned rather than to maintain the crypto–special creation proposition that behavior observed is *directly* determined by the particular DNA of the organism. As Earl Count (1973) has so aptly insisted, we need to distinguish between programmed potential for behavior and programmed behavior—the observed, regularized behavior. The latter constitutes the behavioral continuity that identifies any restricted animal population. I assume, further, that this continuity is a tradition of learned behavior because it does not represent the elicitation of the totality of potential behavior.

The generic tradition of learned behavior in viable hominid groups is culture, by which hominid organisms assume the quality of being human. Culture, then, is that minimal set of socially learned, socially shared, and socially utilized behaviors that ensure the identifiable spatial and temporal continuity of a society. Of course, it is banal to observe that not all individuals learn and use their culture in exactly the same manner. However, it is necessary to indicate that these heuristic processes must follow designated guidelines in order to make certain a society will persist. These guidelines, or models, go by many names, but what is at issue is the structuring of behavior.

It is not my purpose to become embroiled in the structured structure dispute. But another assumption enters here. My characterization of cultural structure posits that the limits of permissible behavior constitute the structure of culture. Within these limits the individual personality is permitted any number of innovations. The range of permissible behavior, which is equal to the number and extent of statuses and roles, varies with the degree of cultural complexity. Hence, propositions derived from the investigation of simpler cultures may not be applicable to complex ones.

Further, what does a society do with behavior that transgresses the permissible bounds? The very presence of unused potential will make for unexpected and unexplained behavior. Along with events that occur unpredictably, unexplained and unexpected actions must be accommodated to the behavior that is within the permissible limits. Here lies the basis of value. To verify satisfactory predictable behavior, the unsatisfactory and unpredictable must be explained. This verification can be done only on a nonempirical basis and, in fact, in terms of absolute truths. With these truths, the members of a society are able to make decisions about the totality of existence. When practiced, the truths constitute the myth of the culture.

There remain some assumptions and propositions about personality. Again, a short definition will suffice. Personality is an individual organism's unique configuration of identifying behavioral characteristics. We shall maintain that the nature of personality, a person's unique behavioral configuration, will be determined by the number of knowledge systems encountered, learned, and utilized by the individual, and that these knowledge systems vary greatly according to the sociocultural complexity involved. Consequently, there should be degrees of personality variation appropriate to the degree of cultural complexity.

This does not imply that individual personalities are not recognizably distinct in any culture, but that the manner in which a culture is acquired by the individual organism correlates with cultural complexity; therefore, with an increase in cultural complexity, an individual's enculturation becomes increasingly distinct from that of all others in that society.

The foregoing involves one of the problems associated with attempts to categorize cultures according to form, levels of integration, and schemes of cultural evolution. By not permitting myself the pleasure of evaluating cultures in this context, I shall spare myself the misery of taking on the terminological morass that accompanies it. Suffice it to say that total culture history does demonstrate an increase in culture content and the complexity of its organization.

It is evident that most of human history has been produced by small societies with much less complexity than obtains in civilizational cultures. Band, tribe, village, chiefdom—whatever the terms, these are the cultural forms wherein the formation of individual personality rests on the emphasis of family, kin, neighborhood, and alliances to enhance them. Early or archaic civilizations presented the first major challenge to those valuing structures by increasing the discreteness of knowledge systems and the modes of using and sharing them. The response to the challenge was paradoxical.

With the emergence of civilization, the primary forms of earlier cultural units were transmuted and adapted to specialized occupations and neighborhoods; at the same time a smaller and smaller proportion of the total culture was within the ken of the individual personality. In addition, because of the difficulty of sharing culture to the degree possible in tribes and villages, overarching structures designed to maintain cohesion appeared: states, state religions, nation-states, and patriotism—not to mention universal religions, when civilizational cultures came in contact with one another.

In early civilizations the human potential for personality development was held in check by the retention of past valuing systems—kin, locality, alliance. Another phenomenon that accompanied man into civilization was the timeless present of ahistorical cultures. Indeed, Eliade's (1961, 104–13) characterization is pertinent: early civilizations attempted to override the implications of writing and its offspring, the discreteness of historical events, through the refusal of history. This remark illustrates how strong the affiliation with earlier cultures was and how great a role they still play in personality formation.

The early civilizations have many survivors in the world today. We need only look to the Mediterranean to find kin, alliance, patron-client, and locality affiliations holding sway. But modern civilization is something new.

Industrial urbanism is a better way of characterizing modern culture, or modern civilization. More than power-driven machine production and the intensification of economic interdependence is important here: industrial urban culture is bound to no particular geographical location. Further, the increasing discreteness of culture history has resulted in many more knowledge systems and the elaboration of statuses and roles.

In modern civilization the older forms of enculturation and social integration are seriously threatened. The result has been the increasing discreteness of culture history and increased individuation of personality. This is very apparent in the scientific method, which is a way of knowing available to all individuals. Its very democracy as a process of knowing enhances the individuality of personality.

To recapitulate, I have proposed that a structural view of human behavioral tradition may be defined as the limits of permissible behavior. Within these limits lies behavior that is human to a given society. Further, these parameters represent attempts to make a statement about the entirety of human existence and of necessity recognize that there is behavior beyond that defined as human. Once human behavior is defined, the basic values by which decisions are made can be derived. Behavior that transgresses the limits of permissible behavior is nonhuman, essentially evil. Finally, the increase in the discreteness of events impels civilizational society toward a conception of linear time: hence the emergence of history and the loss of the eternal present. Given this, civilization implies an infinity of behaviors beyond the permissible limits, for with history the past cannot be repeated.

Whatever conceptualization of structuralism we adopt, structuring presents models of behavior for human groups. Unfortunately, these models are essentially formulations acting as solutions to past problems. Models and structures, once achieved and recognized as human behavior, present an understanding of the past but offer only the most general guidelines for the present and the future. We need them to be human, but we controvert them in daily behavior. These models are our only insurance for the continuity of socialization and enculturation and, thus, society. Their existential modification, however, emphasizes the uniqueness of the present and the future. In this process there is the implicit recognition of behavior beyond present standards. We must again emphasize that because the potential range of behavior is unknown, man is confronted with an infinity of possibilities.

In civilization, and especially modern civilization, the universal if not necessary conservatism of all cultures impels us to look backward to previous circumstance and model. This stance, however, is counterposed by an increase and differentiation in the range of experience and a growing number of increasingly complex knowledge systems.

In modern civilization, cultural complexity and performance are closely related in that there is greater variety and redundancy in both than in simpler modes of cultural life. In civilizational culture the individual personality is forced to a consciousness of infinity in both a temporal and a behavioral sense. Unlike the situation in cultures of lesser complexity, the abstractions of value and myth devolve more and more on the individual as the only means of creating a performance that deals with the totality of experience.

Because of this devolution, it is not a compact of cooperation and mutual obligation that obtains between members of a modern society; it is, obversely, the mutual tolerance of difference that stems from the individuation of personality. We seek conscious compacts that ensure social unity and individual integrity at once. This circumstance impels us not to a view of the past but an accommodation to the present that has no meaning except in permitting the retention and verification of the individual in that salient condition of modern civilization, the future. The civilizational mode is not of a piece. It is a mosaic of individualized experience.

Here one may ask, "Has not the individual always been this human mosaic?" I would agree. At the same time, I would argue that the potential for this mosaic has never been exploited in the manner or to the extent that modern civilization demands. Humankind has always used the past to solve present problems, and their solution has always lain in the future. Until civilization, and particularly modern civilization, however, the past was considered part of the present, and because of this fusion there was little conceptualization of the future. To repeat, humanity's search for the meaning of the totality has always resulted in structurings, in setting limits of permissible behavior, for the purpose of ensuring a high level of predictability of human experience. I argue here that modern civilization, for the reasons briefly alluded to above, blurs these limits and that the increased individuation of personality more readily consigns the limits to obsolescence.

In repeating that the individuation of personality is the companion of growing cultural complexity, I am not proposing that there is any demonstrable difference in the neurological potential between persons in civilization and those in other cultures. My point is that, because of the greater number of roles the individual must play, the convergence of consciousness and social action has become more discrete and intense in modern culture, creating a greater lack of coincidence between the life histories of individual personalities making up a society.

Along with my colleague John L. Fischer, I am of the conviction that the individual personality is a crucial locus of culture (Fischer 1973, 439, 443). I would go further and say that the individual personality is the nexus and praxis of culture. If so, what differentiates human personality in modern culture? It is not that the function of the individual personality vis-à-vis culture is any different in modern civilization; rather, it is that modern culture is so much more extensive that the means of acquiring culture have changed, and that because of these changes the individual must more consciously learn and practice culture. Personalities have always been individualized, but now life histories are increasingly mapped individually. There has been an accelerated loss of shared sex and age grades, and even loss of life crisis rituals and their social assurance—so much so that we are moving toward a time when the only certain shared reference points in social geography are likely to be infancy and senility.

A phenomenological companion of the foregoing trend is the rise of conscious decision-making in the daily life of individuals. Attendant to this behavior is another characteristic process of the individual in civilizational culture: learning to learn. As Earl Count (1967, 51–52) demonstrated, learning to learn increases the separation of the individual from others in his society and promotes a greater self-consciousness. There is a clearer and more pervasive differentiation of self from other and, because of the individual synthesis, a stronger separation of the social self from the secret self.

Given these propositions, can we then entertain the idea that myths and basic values, the emotional cement of most societies, are less and less shared? Or to put it another way, is there the beginning of avoidance of structuring in modern society?

If so, the fact reflects the loss of status and role uniformity I referred to above. Given the changes and choices in life histories that modern culture presents the individual, a social hiatus is developing between infancy and senility. Even though the completion of infancy is indicative of survival, the chances are that little else beyond infancy is shared in society until death.

The subtitle of this paper is a deliberate choice: our shared social life tends more and more to be at the beginning and the end. Infancy and senility in this sense are homologues. Their end points are their extinction: infancy in weaning (see Count 1967), the individual personality in death. Other shared characteristics include physical dependence and the insufficiency of communication (although in senility the latter may come from the refusal as much as the inability of individuals to receive messages).

What is going on in the hiatus? Certainly the ranges of innovation are phenomenologically little different in all cultures: as long as the individual stays within the bounds of permissible behavior, variation can abound. Indeed, the differences between tribal cultures and ancient civilization are not of kind but of degree. Creativity represents another form of individualized focus on culture change. In this phenomenon, essentially a replacement process, different ways of being human displace the previous limits of permissible behavior. With the rise of the importance of the individual personality, I would judge that the opportunities for creativity are greater and more revolutionary than in all past human history. The greater differentiation of individual personalities brings into range a greater emphasis on individual culture.

Are we at the point in human history where the traditional roles we have held as models for the achievement of personality are no longer necessary? Such seemingly universal aspects of life as childhood and adolescence, adulthood and parenthood, male and female seem to be less and less functional in modern civilization.

The recognition of this possibility has led to both intellectual and popular denigration of the results. Popularly, the individuation of personality has been labeled selfishness. I judge this to be a misidentification based on models and values more appropriate to the past. Since Durkheim, a long series of social scientists and philosophers have stressed the alienation of the individual from society, the state of anomie, the sad circumstance of marginal man, and so on.

It is not the process of alienation, nor its condition—anomie—that is significant in this context. What needs to be recognized is that we are in a liminal state, a transforming stage in the evolution of personality. We are participating in the elicitation of new behaviors convergent in the self-conscious personality demanded by modern culture. The condition of anomie is a universal phenomenon; the process of alienation is culture-specific. Sufficiently widespread alienation in a society evokes culture change and, in the historical context, a new organization of personality. My perception is that for the first time in human history, alienation and anomie are universally coincident. We can with some confidence speak of world culture rather than the restricted world of the *Oikumenē*—the known world. All culture is becoming the *Oikumenē*. In the past, an individual undergoing alienation from his own culture sufficient to bring about a state of anomie became a nonhuman isolate in his own society or was forced to seek membership in another, if possible. Because there is decreasing opportunity for the rebel or deviant to migrate to a different culture, the transgressor of the limits of permissible behavior has no ready refuge except the individual personality. Our models of ideal behavior are inadequate and noncommensurate with modern life, despite the desirability and value placed on them. We still attempt to commit ourselves to values—structural models—that we deny behaviorally in our daily lives. In so denying these values, we controvert the only ultimate truths available to society and bring evil into the world.

These propositions have relevance to Lévi-Strauss's (1971) ultimate binary structure: life/death. While positing this polarity as the ultimate one, Lévi-Strauss maintains that there are always intervening structures between the individual on the one hand and the life/death polarity on the other. Given what I have asserted above about modern culture and its intensification of individuation, the individual personality is more blatantly exposed to the polarity than ever before. The life/death polarity is being divested of those intervening structures—the shared roles and statuses of life history, for example—that mask death. Curiously, the modern personality shares with its medieval counterpart the daily presence of death and the unpredictability of social life. Does life become as nothing because once exposed, divested of its social armor, it is not worth living?

In the modern world we seek to construct intervening structures. Needham (1978), in his search for universal processes, suggests solutions to the problems we have been discussing. He conjures a transmutation of the individual's experience into synthetic images activated through evasive fantasies: imagination, myth (metamorphosis), dreams. One might surmise that these processes are consciously employed in the modern world. Even if the movement to the individuation of personality is as great as proposed, could not these processes be used to support the traditional maintenance of personality?

It is difficult to say. An understanding of the relationship between personality and culture in complex cultures, especially civilization, lies in comprehending the extent to which self-conscious modes of realization are forced on the individual. As society becomes a concatenation of "self-conscious" worlds, we shall have to reconsider our conception of culture. Will culture continue to be the unbound variable in human affairs as Colby (1973, 366) has maintained? Will culture continue to mask the life/death polarity from us? Or will individual personality replace it?

Beyond all this, we need to consider whether or not the availability of many knowledge systems impels the individual to make the holistic statements that were formerly in the realm of society's responsibility. If I am correct about modern civilization, a trend toward the individual composition of basic values has been accompanied by a decline in the possibility of social/cultural holism. And if evil is that which lies on the other side of structured behavior, does not the individuation of basic values release evil upon us?

We can speculate further. The foregoing speculation suggests the dominance of individual myths over cultural myths. Given the possibilities of the separate world of personality and its modern enhancement, can we contemplate the loss of cultural beings and the end of cultural man? For as the individual personality, the functioning synthesis of knowledge and experience, comes to dominate conscious life, so then do the individual personalities share less and less socially. Or is the change we are observing merely the continuous expansion in the elicitation of human potential? Are the past models of human being truly unserving in the present?

As I make these mild queries, I realize that I may have been writing about anthropologists all along. The *fieldworking* cultural anthropologist becomes indeed the world as the individual, and with a vengeance. The cultural process and the individual anthropologist are coordinate, for to approximate a cross-cultural view, he or she must in effect create a new culture. Furthermore, there is a parallel between the subjectivism of the individuation of personality and one of the primary characteristics of anthropologists. We are mythmakers. *Pace* Richardson (1975). *Pace* Lévi-Strauss (1971, 611).

Having elicited behavior that trespasses the limits of the permissible as delineated in our culturally inherited models of human being, we can only self-consciously construct a personality that ignores the past, but in the process we have not become capable of dealing with the seeming infinity of possible behaviors. The management of infinity, then, becomes the conscious task of all personalities that partake of modern culture.

We are become our own world.

We are become our own evil.

Alternation of Logical Fields: Preadaptation for Civilization

JOSEPH V. GUILLOTTE III

This essay focuses upon the flexibility that is required in human behavior with specific emphasis upon the strains of maneuvering in a civilization. I begin with a description of a religious occasion in a Tanzanian tribe, then present a definition of religion that seems to accommodate this event, and discuss an aspect of this definition: the manipulation or alternation of logical fields. Such manipulation, I suggest, is crucial for survival at all technological levels.

I heard of what at first appeared to be an insignificant event while I was carrying out research in northern Tanzania in 1970. My fieldwork concentrated on describing and analyzing a multiethnic community called Magugu, a settlement founded in 1944—by order of the British colonial government—about ninety miles southwest of Arusha, on the Great North Road, the main north-south traffic artery of Tanzania. After an outbreak of sleeping sickness (trypanosomiasis rhodesiensis) on European-owned estates to the south, about 1,000 volunteers from the work forces of these estates were settled in what came to be the Magugu area. These pioneers were given lodging, food, medical care, and farmland in return for clearing brush to halt the advance of the tsetse fly, the vector of the disease. The original volunteers, and other farmers who migrated subsequently, came from all over East Africa; more than eighty tribal groups appeared in the various samples and censuses that I conducted. Local lore has it that in the Magugu population there are 120 tribes, a number derived from the belief that there are 100 tribal groups in the nation of Tanzania. Magugu people see their community as a microcosm of the nation, a place where ethnic diversity is homogenized over time.

The first settlers of Magugu were situated in virtually empty bush.

Although the land was unoccupied, the Mbugwe tribe, who at the time lived around the southern shore of Lake Manyara (about ten miles north of the site of Magugu), claimed the territory. The Mbugwe were not farming the land that was to be used by the newcomers, but they had hunted there and gathered wild plants and firewood.

From the beginning, the Mbugwe and the settlers were at odds. The settlers were migrants in a strange land and feared the Mbugwe as formidable sorcerers and owners of the land. The Mbugwe looked upon the settlers as antipathetic to them religiously, politically, economically, and socially. The majority of the Mbugwe were pagan or nominally Catholic; the settlers were preponderantly Moslem. The Mbugwe were organized in a chiefdom imposed by the British; the settlers were under the aegis of an elected headman who was, in theory, subservient to the Mbugwe Paramount Chief. The Mbugwe were pastoralists and cultivators of millet; the settlers were small farmers who cultivated plots of maize and wet rice. The Mbugwe were organized into matrilineal clans; the settlers, as a rule, focused the intensity of their social relations upon the nuclear family, since they were often solitary migrants in a community of migrants and had no extended circle of kinfolk in Magugu.

The event that stimulated this essay occurred at a Mbugwe *sadaka*. In the context used here, this Swahili term means the secondary funeral sacrifice and feast that takes place about a year after the death of an individual. Prior to the feast, the deceased's spirit is believed to be in a transitory state, and such a ceremony is considered absolutely necessary for his entry into the country of the dead and his permanent residence there. Failure to conduct such propitiation will incite the spirit to severely harass his living descendants. Catholic Mbugwe often justify the ceremony in light of Christian theology and say that a *sadaka* is like a holy day to pray for the departed so that he might enter heaven. In this particular case, a Catholic Mbugwe had gone to great expense to provide a ritual feast for his pagan father's spirit.

Large quantities of beer were brewed, several goats and cows were purchased, and invitations were extended to lineal and affinal relatives and to neighbors. Some seventy guests, about equally divided between pagan and Catholic Mbugwe, gathered for the dancing and feasting. Two Moslem Mbugwe were also welcomed as kinsmen and joined in the beer drinking and dancing. An ecumenical spirit prevailed until the moment arrived for slaughtering the livestock for the feast.

The traditional Mbugwe method for killing domesticated animals is strangulation with a rawhide thong. The two Moslem Mbugwe vociferously decried the custom, arguing that as Moslems they were forbidden to eat any animal that had not been killed by cutting its throat. They threatened not only to refuse the meal but to leave the feast. The Catholic host conferred with his *mwendiokwia,* the man who had positionally succeeded his father, and they agreed to placate the dissenters; the animals would be killed by having their throats slit. With that, harmony was restored; the animals were butchered and cooked, and the feasting began.

Neither Moslems nor Christians at this feast saw any difficulty in taking part in a ceremony based on postulates different from the structuring of the unknown in their respective religions. Perhaps the availability of plentiful beer and meat dampened the fervor of the more orthodox. At any rate, the social gathering convened to propitiate ancestral spirits was not interrupted until a secondary tenet of Islam was about to be violated. By deciding to stress their religion in protesting a relatively inconsequential transgression, rather than in refusing to attend the feast at all, the two Moslem Mbugwe demonstrated that tribal ceremonies can be manipulated by individuals and groups to conform to a variety of concepts about the supernatural.

The *sadaka* incident calls for a definition of religion that accounts for seeming inconstancy of behavior. I suggest that religion is a process that individuals and groups use to structure the unknown. It involves the creation and use of symbols, actions, and organizations, and it often requires the manipulation of more than one logical field at the same time or within a short span of time. Its function is the provision of relief from personal and social tension and crisis, and it provides some degree of explanation for the unforeseen. The unknown is the supernatural: that is, what is not defined as scientific or natural in terms of the group's or individual's world view.

A logical field is a set of components (symbols, actions, or organizations) arranged in such a manner that contradictions are avoided. Logical fields are sets or arrays of interrelated data. What is contradictory or noncontradictory is, naturally, culturally relative and often ephemeral. A logical field is related to roles and other forms of situational behavior. Gearing's term "structural poses" comes close to my intent: that is, "a series of several sets of roles and groups which appear and disappear according to the tasks at hand" (Gearing 1974, 181). The participation of an individual or group in a logical field may be conscious or unconscious; it requires concentration upon a "task at hand" and—as a corollary—the suppression of other, contradictory data. Humans seem to have the ability to enter an almost trancelike state in order to ignore extraneous data. Certainly, play—the human (and mammalian) propensity to disassemble and reassemble the immediately manipulable environment—is a progenitor and perpetuator of this human capacity. The concept of a logical field can be related to something so minute as a grammatical utterance or so grand as expectations concerning ethnicity and national character.

In essence, I have labeled logical fields those mechanisms by which humans define and redefine the terms of their existence. With such a mechanism, contradictory information and situations can be assimilated, ignored, or recast. The particular occasion which I discuss is religious, but by no means are logical fields exclusively religious. I do suspect that religion is an area where humans tend to actively manipulate logical fields, but we do the same in the economic sphere as new definitions of reciprocity and partnership develop; and in politics as alliances shift, friends become enemies, and strangers become friends. Often these shifts involve alternation of logical fields of this order: "A is a member of group X; therefore he is an enemy" changes to "A is a member of group X; therefore he is a friend."

The concept of manipulating several logical fields requires some explanation, since it is crucial to the definition of religion and specific to the general discussion of the topic of logical fields. The kernel of the idea comes from Robert Bellah's article "Religious Evolution." He stated that religious systems can be classified in five broad stages: Primitive, Archaic, Historic, Early Modern, and Modern. He sees evolution as "a process of increasing differentiation and complexity of organization which endows the organism, social system, or whatever the unit in question may be, with greater capacity to adapt to its environment than were its less complex ancestors" (Bellah 1965, 75). He does not posit any irreversibility, inevitability, or commitment to any particular course in this process; in fact, all levels of evolutionary development can exist side by side. In the Mbugwe *sadaka* we can observe Bellah's monistic Primitive stage of religious evolution in which the supernatural permeates the fabric of the social structure, and the ancestral spirits are privy to the most intimate of human affairs. In Christianity and Islam, we can also perceive the dualistic embodiment of gods and saints completely separated from humankind and only imperfectly contacted through intermediaries.

An event such as the *sadaka* indicates that diversity of cosmic construction can be observed within the same individual or group at the same time, or within a short span of time. For example, a person who practices magic visualizes a monistic system as the logical structure of the universe. That individual sees the whole universe as comprising forces that are functionally integrated. The application of a formula to one part of the system causes reverberations that bring about predictable effects in another part of the system. The juxtaposition of certain components of a magical formula will cause certain results because the whole universe is interconnected and unified. Metaphorically, it is a "domino theory" of the cosmos.

In contrast to this monistic structure, a Christian or Moslem believes in a dualistic universe, a separation of the real world from the supernatural. The latter is only imperfectly approached by individuals and groups, who, at best, mediate the two sectors. I would interpret the different roles and attitudes of the shaman and priest in this light. The shaman manipulates and controls the supernatural; the priest supplicates or beseeches the supernatural (Hoebel 1966, 469). These different attitudes presuppose monistic and dualistic constructs of the universe. They may be held by the same individual and reconciled by his manipulation of or (perhaps more properly) alternation between two logical fields. What type of cosmic structure is conceived by a Catholic Mbugwe who believes in magic? Having met many such individuals, I propose that they, like many other humans, are able and even eager to switch back and forth from one logical field to another.

This switching can be done within any area—social organization, economics, or politics. Humans may have to vacillate in their logical fields and maintain inconsistency in order to survive, or at least to stay sane. Such vacillation can be exemplified in the multilingualism that is the norm in Magugu. Learning another language involves the separation of the logical field of the first language from that of the second.

Using two languages then involves switching from one logical field to another. Except for a few elders, all the Mbugwe I observed did this every day between their own vernacular and Swahili. Extending this argument from religious and linguistic categories to a pan-cultural framework, one might infer that social and cultural change occur because of the human ability and, indeed, propensity to alternate logical fields.

Orr and Cappanari suggest that the capacity to alternate between logical fields may be part of the neuroanatomical process of human evolution that preadapted us for speech. They contend that language may well have been a corollary or epiphenomenon implicit in evolutionary change, like the advantageous growth of cortical control over fine movement of the fingers. Because of the already present basic intrinsic patterns of neuronal arrangements, they believe that this control was accomplished by a complex system of suppressor and inhibitory networks involving also the lips, tongue, and larynx. This change, which was the precursor of articulate speech, may have had no apparent survival value at the time. They make the further point that control of articulate speech is an inhibitory rather than an excitory phenomenon, that the cortical evolution leading to language involved the development of restrictive and constraining neurophysiological mechanisms rather than the addition of new efferent motor pathways. Humans are able to select a few out of the many potential sounds for articulate speech only because they can selectively inhibit the emission of irrelevant noise (Orr and Cappanari 1964, 318–24).

I suggest that the evolutionary ability to suppress and screen out stimuli and to internally inhibit synapses are preadaptations to civilization. Civilization is multiethnic and multifaceted, a collectivity in which symbols of diverse—often contradictory—meaning and origin are thrown together. To function as civilized people, to operate in the face of so many opposing creeds, options, and opportunities, we first had to evolve the ability to reduce the universe to manageable terms. LeMay suggests that this ability, exemplified by the acquisition of language, was well established by Neanderthal times; certainly, it long preceded the rise of civilization (LeMay 1975, 9–14). The "thought" system called logic is a further manifestation of inhibitory processes. By avoiding contradictions, we are able to sweep under the rug large amounts of symbolic and operational institutional detritus at any one time. We succeed in a civilization through the suppression of data and experience. One connotation of the word "civilized" refers to the ability to adroitly handle contradictory logical fields. Indeed, Freud, whose *Civilization and Its Discontents* provides the title for this volume, spoke of an "organic repression" paving the way to civilization (Strachey 1962, 6). He is certainly convincing in his argument that civilization produces cultural frustration (Freud 1962, 49). We can avoid considerable frustration, however, by switching logical fields.

Much of traditional law involves alternation between logical fields, as Comaroff and Roberts imply in a recent study of Tswana law. The Tswana, like the Mbugwe and ourselves, live in a fluid universe. They constantly face value opposition and its expression in the two domains of agnation and matrilaterality. Men tend to seek early alliances with unrelated partners and later marriages with kin. Since unions with agnates are progressively more difficult to redefine because they also become affines, these marriages typically involve the growth of pragmatic constraints on the strategic manipulation of ambiguity. The subtle equation involved in *sustaining and eliminating ambiguity* is one that most Tswana face at some point (Comaroff and Roberts 1981, 61, 65; my emphasis). In disputes, opposing Tswana draw upon a normative repertoire to legitimize competing constructions of reality. In adjudication before a headman or chief, the mediator "may order his decision within the agreed paradigm, choose between the rival ones, or impose a fresh paradigm on the issues under dispute" (Comaroff and Roberts 1981, 74, 85).

Hockett and Ascher's discussion of the "opening" of a primate call system helps clarify the ability of humans to evolve symbols and vary their meaning. "Let us represent the acoustic contours of one inherited call arbitrarily with the sequence of letters ABCD and those of another with EFGH. All we mean by either of these representations is that each call possesses two or more acoustic properties on which primate ears could focus attention; it does not matter just how many such acoustic properties are involved nor just what they are. Suppose that ABCD means 'food here,' while EFGH means 'danger coming.' Finding both food and danger, the hominid comes out with ABGH. If this new call becomes established, then the two old calls and the new one are all henceforth composite, instead of unanalyzable unitary signals. For in ABCD, the part AB now means 'food' and the part CD means 'no danger'; in EFGH, EF now means 'no food' and GH means 'danger'; while ABGH means 'food and danger' because AB and GH have acquired the meanings just mentioned. One might eventually even get EFCD, obviously meaning 'no food and no danger' " (Hockett and Ascher 1968, 337).

Applying this analysis to ethnographic data, we can posit that after the *sadaka* ceremony earlier described, participants could no longer define the sacrifice as *requiring* the strangulation of livestock. Rather, the symbolic logical system had been "opened" so that *sadaka* would have to be defined thereafter as involving *either* strangulation *or* cutting the animal's throat. Alternation of logical fields would allow supplicants to operate in the traditional manner and yet to follow the Islamic method of slaughter insofar as it suited their purposes. With such a choice in religious maneuvering, the individual is able to adapt to a multicultural environment like that in Magugu.

I suggest that Hockett and Ascher's views on the process of "opening" a system also occurs in what we call pidginization and creolization. The "marginal" languages that arise as makeshift adaptations are reduced in structure and use, compared with the first languages of speakers in a region; there are "universal tendencies to adapt speech and varieties of a language, by *simplification* in some circumstances, *expansion* in others," and language contact gives rise to "a *partial confluence* of linguistic traditions" (Hymes 1974, 3, 9; my emphasis). Decamp maintains that as many grammatical devices are eliminated, a drastic reduction of redundant factors occurs (Decamp 1974, 15). A characteristic of pidgins that suggests the practicality of the alternation of logical fields is their limitation and specialization: "If the interlingual contact ends, the pidgin usually also ends; there is no longer a need for it, and there are no sentimental attachments or nationalistic motivations for preserving a dead pidgin" (Decamp 1974, 16). In other words, once the matter at hand is completed, the pidgin can be discarded. Obviously, the pidginization process is sometimes necessary to the setting up of logical fields in a multicultural situation. We should note, however, that such blending processes can also be relevant to the shattering of one logical field and the creation of another.

Politicians are usually expert in shifting and alternating logical fields. The Magugu Tanganyika African National Union Chairman, who had been in office since the national political party was organized in the community in 1956, seemed to be part of each religious community. He attended Catholic Mass, he wore a Moslem *kofia* or pillbox cap, and he kept close ties with both traditional curers and Protestant congregations. When I tried to pin him down as to his religious affiliation, he mumbled something about being interested in all religions.

I have suggested that the shifting of logical fields is a human means of avoiding contradiction. As long as appropriate rules are applied—that is, performance of certain actions within certain frames—humans seem able to handle considerable contradiction without undue psychic stress. People as nonviolent as the Semai, for example, can function as soldiers and counterinsurgents *outside* their own society (Dentan 1968, 81).

But part of the burden of being civilized is that individuals and groups cannot always effect such alternation. The ability to suppress data is sometimes limited, and the inability to manipulate logical fields can push the individual and society to the brink of dysfunction—madness for the individual, disorganization for the society.

Some people refuse to ignore the existence of another logical field or to shift situationally from one to another. One such person is Frank Serpico, a New York city policeman who persisted in *not* shifting from one logical field to another to please his superiors or fellow officers. When he was transferred to a South Bronx precinct where the other officers had been corrupted by drug dealers, he eventually discovered that he was the only policeman not "on the pad." When he subsequently testified against the others, he was denigrated and despised by his former comrades. Another example is Colonel Anthony Herbert, whose book *Soldier* relates his own intransigence in the face of bureaucratic pressure from the United States Army during the Vietnam War. He persisted in pressing charges of atrocity and war crimes in the face of an apparent cover-up by his superiors.

These men did not play the game their peers and superiors thought they should. They really believed in the mythic system that they were taught in their childhood and in the instruction they had received as police officer and soldier. They made no distinction between the logical field of ideal culture and that of real culture (Maas 1973; Herbert with Wooten 1973). History is full of such individuals, who are either branded as fools or acclaimed as heroes, depending on the point of view of the analyst. As civilization brings pressure to bear upon groups and individuals to alternate between logical fields, the choices of fields within which to maneuver can be so numerous that we become confused, sometimes to the point of drawing upon the ultimate inhibitory process—total retreat from all logical fields.

I encountered the Mbugwe in 1969–70, when they saw themselves as tribal and were seen by others, such as the Moslem settlers, as benighted and retrogressive—primitive anachronisms in a newly independent country. Yet for decades their lives had been affected by such forces as German and British colonial governments and the ensuing government of independent Tanzania; the Swahili lingua franca, which ultimately became the national language of Tanzania; World War I campaigns in their homeland; labor migration; the world religions of Christianity and Islam; multitudes of foreign immigrants from various parts of Europe, as well as people from other tribal areas of Africa; new crops and new technology. In sum, the Mbugwe did not live in isolation or in a vacuum. Although they scarified their faces, wore togalike garments, and carried spears, for over seventy years they had been aware of the forces that were forming East African civilization.

The Moslem and multiethnic community of Magugu contrasts with the tribal and multireligious Mbugwe. In a sense they belong to different time spans. The Mbugwe are representatives of hundreds of African mixed-farming groups that through the centuries adapted to their environments with a simple technology and complex social system. The Magugu settlement is a product of colonial Africa as well as the Africa of independent nation-states. It is a product of a time when people could move about without the protection of large kin groups and of a time when a cash economy dictated that individuals move hundreds of miles to secure employment at plantations, mines, or factories. Although the Magugu settlers came from societies not too different from that of the Mbugwe, they had to slough off or set aside their primary ethnic roles or ethnic logical fields when they arrived at Magugu. In such a heterogeneous settlement they began the process of homogenization by creating new types of logical fields, with Islam as a base for setting up lines of communication across previously impenetrable cultural barriers.

Although the Mbugwe were flexible in adjusting to religious variants in the *sadaka,* they are not seen as such in other areas of interaction with the wider civilization of Tanzania. Their resistance to socialistic dogma and practice, and their refusal to mingle with others in the neighborhood either through intermarriage or residency are but two of a number of social lapses for which they are indicted by the Magugu settlers and leaders, who are more closely aligned with the national government. The affinity for nation is one in which the people of Magugu are placed by default: they are by no means ardent patriots or socialist theoreticians, but since they have no extensive tribal or cultural networks, they must perforce cleave to national language, national politics, and a world religion.

Antipathies and adjustments between ethnic groups occupying their own homeland and unassimilable outsiders who have settled near or amidst them has probably been the rule for thousands of years. Certainly, we can imagine such a situation occurring during the formation of an early city-state—Ur, or Akkad, or Uxmal. Since the state and civilization are almost by definition multiethnic, we can envisage the increasing complexity of logical fields and the shattering and recombinations of those fields as diverse peoples were forced into proximity. The extent to which this old human strategy can continue to function is uncertain. Population figures suggest that by the year 2000 there will be six billion people on earth—six billion different vantage points from which to view the universe, six billion generators of logical fields. We can perhaps extrapolate from the past that myriads of logical fields can be constantly revised and that most humans will continue to manipulate them. Yet a possible scarcity of resources raises the grim prospect of humans withdrawing into themselves and abandoning all social contact.

My final comment derives from another sojourn in an African city in 1979, where I was a consultant on a nutritional intervention team assessing protein energy malnutrition among infants. The high incidence of *kwashiorkor* and marasmus in this area prompted the team to question mothers about infant illness and compare their responses with statistical information on infant deaths in the largest hospital in the country. The equivalency of folk and medical statistics was amazing. African mothers knew exactly what caused infant illness and death and, furthermore, knew the symptoms of the ten major causes of death. Then why were children permitted to reach such extreme conditions of debilitation? Mothers who, in the aggregate, knew practically everything there was to know about childhood illness claimed as individuals that they did not recognize the symptoms of malnutrition. When I saw a three-year-old girl weighing seven kilos, I asked why the mother had not brought the child to the hospital sooner. She answered that she did not know the child was sick. I later suggested to team members that we were observing infanticide. We were also observing a darker side of the convenient suppression of cultural data and the manipulation of logical fields. The extremity of this development might well be the inability of many of our species even to recognize what is contradictory, much less attempt to avoid it.

Why Our Civilization Can Never Be "Moral": The Cultural Ecology of Christian Origins

MALCOLM C. WEBB

It is evident that the powerful effect of religious belief in controlling and motivating behavior and the readiness with which institutionalized religious organizations may become loci for the accumulation and control of wealth have commonly led to the use of religion as a tool of economic and political oppression in class-stratified societies. It is equally obvious that organized Christianity is no exception to this rule. It is also the case, however, that religious institutions have not infrequently served as mechanisms of resistance to oppression. This essay examines the way in which the capacity to resist became a significant feature of our own evolving Judeo-Christian tradition. It concentrates upon the manner in which attitudes of resistance to ruling elites that developed within the context of one national religious tradition—in ancient Israel and postexilic Judaism—became detached from a specific ethnicity and freed to function in a pannational, multiethnic, mass religion.

Even a cursory perusal of the history of Western civilization during the last two millennia supports the contention that the Judeo-Christian ethos has provided a permanent stimulus of and a relatively safe locus—at times the only reasonably secure locus—for radical criticism of social, ethnic, economic, and political elites. Despite the all too frequently oppressive attitudes and actions of the institutional churches and the gross religious conflicts that have characterized certain periods of our history (most currently in Northern Ireland), the long sequence of religion-based rebellions of the masses—extending from the medieval peasants who marched against their lords to the chant of "When Adam delved and Eve span, who was then the gentleman?" through the radical sectarians of the Reformation, the religious left of the English Civil Wars, the nineteenth-century abolitionist movement, the witness against Hitler by both Lutheran clergy and conservative Catholic aristocrats, and the American civil rights movement, to the antiwar and antinuclear movements and the Polish national resistance of the present day—suggests that certain aspects of this religious tradition provide a powerful mechanism, at times a sort of socio-ideological dynamite, by which otherwise powerless and disorganized groups can confront the oppressive features of European capitalist state systems (cf. White 1959).

A decade ago I presented the thesis that by a process of secularization in the eighteenth and nineteenth centuries, which removed its more obviously supernaturalistic and teleological features, this same Judeo-Christian world view helped to give birth to concepts of progressive, systemic, and functional social change that in turn formed important components of both the emerging anthropological perspective and Marxism (Webb 1969; 1973). In the same way, Lynn White has suggested that the introduction into Europe—by way of "the astonishing Jewish heresy called Christianity"—of concern for the lower orders, along with concepts of progressive historical development and the roots of a "natural theology" approach to physical reality, contributed critically to the commercial, scientific, and egalitarian orientation characteristic of that area and placed these values at the very evolutionary, functional core of Western civilization (White 1968, 33ff.; 1958). The result of this long-standing yet ever-changing critical stance has been that no matter how much ruling groups may wish to justify their favored position, to persuade the lower orders—and themselves—that their role as masters is just, moral, and God-given (or, in the terms of supposedly secular and objective science, is the inevitable order of nature and society), a contrary tradition waits ready to spring up and say that it simply isn't so. Clearly, then, we are dealing with a powerful ideological force—or concatenation of forces. What is needed is the specification of the underlying sociocultural causes that led to its formation and spread.

From the point of view of cultural ecology, religion is a mechanism of social, political, and economic integration and mobilization that, although obviously capable of acting as a more or less independent force, must be analyzed in terms of other, more "basic" aspects of the cultural system. Several years ago, in a paper entitled "How the Hebrews Invented the Idea of God," I related the emergence of the concept of historical, ethical, salvationist, radical monotheism to various economic, political, and ethnic conflicts—both internal and external—that took place in the emerging ancient Hebrew kingdoms (Webb 1976). Briefly, it was argued that from a beginning scarcely different from the monolatry of Akhenaten or the concern with a god of causation, which seems to have been general in northern Syria and Mesopotamia at the start of the Iron Age (the name "Yahweh" may be derived from a verbal phrase associated with the Canaanite god "El" in the sense of "El, bringing into existence . . ." various things), the Israelites' god, as the chief god of the evolving confederacy and early monarchy, became the guarantor through time of the developing political and moral order. The god's particular concern for the well-being of the lower orders of society appears in turn to have been a reflection on the one hand of the class oppression imposed by the Davidic dynasty upon the rural commoner population, and on the other of the somewhat later native resistance movement against foreign (Phoenician) domination, a movement largely led by such spokesmen for the less urban, non-elite elements of the population as Elijah, Elisha, Amos, and Hosea.

These developments seem to have first reached fruition in the northern kingdom, both because the absence there of a firmly established dynasty allowed greater scope for rural opposition and because its more prosperous urban character and greater foreign contact created greater stress (cf. Landay 1971, 157–76; Cornfeld and Freedman 1976, 106–26). In this latter situation it would be especially likely that the gods symbolic of ethnic and political identity would be transformed into standards of class loyalty. Indeed, if one accepts the views of Mendenhall (1973) and McKenzie (1966) that the so-called Exodus and Conquest of the thirteenth century B.C. were in reality largely a revolt of the commoner population of rural Palestine against their Egyptian client king overlords, with the rejection of the latter's gods a symbolic statement of the rejection of their right to rulership, then this pro-peasant and anti-elite bias—based at least in part upon ethnic conflict—was an essential aspect of Yahwism from its inception (Bright 1972, 126–39; Anderson 1975, 118–31).

As indicated, from an anthropological perspective these ethical concerns are a reflection of a nativistic movement. The question that must now be addressed is how these concerns, associated with one ethnic group in opposition to all outsiders, became transformed into a multiethnic, pan-European missionary religion. The Sioux did not, for example, send ghost-dance missionaries to Chicago, nor did the cargo cultists preach to the British residents of New Guinea. While the situation is not quite comparable, since a clash of missionary religions is involved, one may also note that the Mahdist and more recent Islamic revitalization movements have not concerned themselves with converting dominating outsiders but rather with eliminating them from the local scene as quickly as possible. Because the change in question is historically associated with the emergence of Christianity and its hiving off from Judaism, what is required is nothing more nor less than a cultural ecology of Christian origins.

Since space precludes detailed attention to questions of New Testament criticism here, we will rely upon currently widely accepted views as to the formation of the various texts and the social circumstances that lie behind them (the *Sitz im Leben*) as these issues have been clarified in such standard and readily available studies and handbooks as those of Bultman (1951–1955; 1968; 1980), Conzelmann (1973a; 1973b), Enslin (1956a; 1956b), Grant (1957), Kee, Young, and Froehlich (1973), Lace (1965), Moule (1965; 1982), Neill (1966), Perrin (1974), Scott (1951), and Throckmorton (1967). My own understanding of the social background and intellectual development of the apostle Paul, clearly a critical figure, has been shaped by the study of Selby (1962), supplemented by Keck (1979) and Sandmel (1958; 1960).

Even with this simplification, any attempt at the reconstruction of the social background of emerging Christianity—whether focusing on the career and teaching of its founder, upon the development of the initial Palestinian church, upon the spread of the movement to Hellenistic Judaism both inside and outside of Palestine, or upon the shift of the locus of the community into the wider Gentile world during the forties and fifties of the first century and later—is fraught with great difficulty. Despite a few extra-biblical references (Dunkerley 1957; Duling 1979, 4–10), the only really extensive evidence is the literature of the New Testament itself—a corpus of material which, although fairly copious even by the standards of classical Greco-Roman and early Jewish writings of the same period, consists of faith statements from a living, worshiping community whose modes of reasoning, methods of exposition, and standards of historical and biographical accuracy were far from those of the modern world. Consequently, contemporary social science must attempt to specify processes and events lying, as it were, "behind" this literature produced by persons whose interests (the advance of a faith they *knew* to be true) and whose sense of causation (the will of God acting through history and now especially in His divinely certified agent, Jesus) are not especially useful for secular historical and cultural analysis.

It is, for example, generally recognized that the career and teaching of Jesus must be reconstructed—insofar as this is possible—from gospel accounts strongly skewed, perhaps unconsciously, by the goals of demonstrating both that Jesus was the Son of God and that he was consciously aware of this fact during his ministry; of relieving the Roman authorities of major responsibility for the crucifixion; and of putting into the mouth of Jesus statements relative to the religious needs of churches in the latter half of the first century. In the same way, although the stress on overtly supernatural activity is much less in the Acts of the Apostles, and although the Pauline and other epistles are—except for various confusions in the texts and some accidental or deliberate misattributions of authorship—reasonably straightforward historically, the former does represent an idealized portrait biased by the author's theological viewpoint, and the latter were occasional works in which most of the social setting and other background are simply assumed. Fortunately, recent decades have witnessed a growing number of studies of the sociology (if not quite the social anthropology) of the setting in which the Jesus movement emerged, among which the work of Edwards (1981), Gager (1975), Hengel (1974a; 1983), Kee (1980), Kundsin (1962), Malherbe (1977), Meeks (1983), and Theissen (1978) have been especially helpful.

Perhaps the first point to be noted is that by the last century B.C., contact between the Jews and the surrounding Gentile world had been extensive, if not always happy—with the result not only that there were large numbers of non-Jewish fellow travelers associated with many of the synagogues of the eastern Mediterranean, kept out of Judaism by the rigors of the evolving Law (and especially in the case of males by the requirement of circumcision), but also that many Greco-

Roman customs and concepts had entered Judaism itself, both in the Diaspora and—strongly—in Palestine (Hengel 1974b and 1980; Kee 1980, 37–42; Selby 1962, 43–58; Stone 1973). In other words, both socially and ideologically, Judaism was in a sense poised to become—or give birth to—a major mass religious movement in the Roman world.

Within this broader setting, Palestine itself was not a happy land. Although some members of the elite—and especially the greater merchants and all classes of the Temple establishment—were doing moderately well, a succession of droughts, epidemics, and other natural disasters had led to agricultural distress and famine, apparently intensified by overpopulation and a lack of land suitable for further agricultural intensification. In addition, the Herodian dynasty had alienated large tracts of land for its own use and that of its hangers-on, and had also encouraged the ongoing process of establishment of Greek cities about the borders of the country. As a result, the economic and social problems inherent in a system of latifundia and absentee landlords had become severe. Another pressure point was the extensive cost of the rebuilding of the Temple and the other elaborate public works undertaken by Herod the Great. Finally, the presence of the monarchy (or, later, the tetrarchs), the Temple bureaucracy, and the Roman imperial system (although the local Roman military establishment was in fact quite small at that time) meant that the population was burdened with three parallel taxation systems. In addition to the usual conflict of interest between rich and poor, then, the small farmers and petty craftsmen—the middling levels of society—were set against the great magnates; and the cities, especially Jerusalem, rich on the profits of the pilgrimage system and sucking in the wealth of the countryside both directly and indirectly, were placed in opposition to the rural areas (Hengel 1974a, 15–20, 28; Jeremias 1972, 74–76 and 1975; Theissen 1978, 35–56).

All the parties of first-century Jewish Palestine can in fact be related to these stresses. The Sadducees, obviously, were the Temple establishment, dependent upon strict observation of religious rules and the preservation of the Roman peace. The Herodians were both the apex and the beneficiaries of the local elite system and also the agents of Roman rule—not an entirely enviable position. The Pharisees were a lay group, in principle opposed to both the monarchy and the political pretensions of the priesthood. Yet because their zeal for the Law inevitably pushed the leadership of the movement into the hands of those relatively wealthy urbanites able to maintain ritual purity and to support the Temple system, the Pharisees increasingly were forced into an uneasy alliance with the Sadducees. The Zealots and daggermen were the resistance parties, striking from their rural bases against both the Romans and the urban wealthy. The Essenes, who had turned against the national leadership in the dispute over the proper appointment of the high priest and other leaders of the religious system, were agriculturally based theocratic communists who had largely withdrawn from the system into rural areas, where they lived in physical and ceremonial isolation (Jeremias 1975, 87ff.; Russell 1968, 28–39, 48–57).

The Jesus movement was in no sense an exception to the generalization that every party took its distinctive stance according to its place in the conflicts noted above. An interesting prior consideration, however, is that all these groups, by attacking the purity and correctness of their opponents' Jewishness, were heading toward the conclusion that "true" Jewishness was not—or not alone—a matter of birth and nationality (Theissen 1978, 93). The conflicts of these interest groups—whose active adherents were actually quite few, relative to the total population (Russell 1968, 48)—together with the small size of the Roman occupying force, left the rural population (the *Am ha-aretz,* or people of the land) pretty much on their own. Since their inability to keep the ritual law (because of poverty and ignorance) led them to be ignored or held in contempt by the Pharisees (otherwise the most nationally conscious and socially concerned of any of the ideological groups), the countryside was left with severely weakened institutions of local leadership—a condition specified by Valentine (1963) as critical to the appearance of millenarian revival movements. An interpretation of Jesus as a nativistic leader therefore seems appropriate.

Although the most authentic strands of the tradition concerning Jesus express considerable hostility toward the national leadership and skepticism toward the Law, and seem also to adhere to the contemporary practice of couching messianic statements in terms of the old Israelite monarchy, and although a prediction of an imminent end of the world brought about by an avenging God and His agent, the Son of Man, rather obviously boded no good for the establishment, Cullmann (1970) and especially Hengel (1971) have rather effectively squelched the idea that Jesus' goals were primarily or effectively political in the modern sense (see, however, Harris 1975, 180–94 for a contrary view). The Temple complex, including the portion devoted to the sale of sacrificial animals, was a very elaborate and physically secure place (Landay 1971, 228–33), the serious seizure of which would have taken an armed force so large as perhaps to have set off the Jewish revolt thirty-five years ahead of time; certainly, it would not have escaped the notice of contemporary historians. The overturning of the money-changers' tables, the Palm Sunday entrance into the city, and perhaps even the references to swords (very likely carried simply for personal protection) are therefore probably best understood as a kind of demonstration or acted-out sermon in the manner of the Old Testament prophets. This is not to say that Jesus did not expect—and hope to help to bring about—a real, physical deliverance from real oppressors (cf. Cornfeld and Freedman 1976, 286–87), or that he was not executed as a seditionist. Crucifixion, one of the most secure elements of the gospel accounts and one utterly unlikely to have been brought into the narrative for any symbolic or theological purpose (Hengel 1977), was specifically mandated for sedition. It is simply to point out that Jesus evidently expected his goals to occur by means other than human agency and that his activities are therefore to be interpreted more in terms of the categories of Mooney (1967), Worsley (1968), Schwartz (1971), or Lanternari (1963) than as what we would understand as political action.

The structure of the movement that focused upon Jesus, insofar as this can be deduced, also supports this characterization. Gerd Theissen, in a brilliant and widely influential application of form criticism (Theissen 1978; cf. Edwards 1981; Kundsin 1962; Perrin 1974, 42–54, 72–79), has pointed out that Palestinian Christianity in its earliest stage—during the 30s and 40s—consisted of two wings. The first was an organized community centered on the Jerusalem apostles, which in time produced such narrative materials as St. Mark's gospel (or perhaps the pericopes that were used in its later composition). The other appears to have been a collection of wandering charismatic preachers moving among small village groups in the rural areas, especially Galilee, delivering in the name of the founder and bearer of revelation, Jesus, those aphoristic and apodictic moral judgments, wisdom statements, and predictions of the *Eschaton* that we know as the "Q source," a document presumed lost shortly after its incorporation into Matthew and Luke. Since the situation suggested in Acts and the Pauline epistles clearly shows a shifting from the latter to the former, we may project the charismatic pattern back to Jesus' own mission; whether the wandering preachers faithfully copied Jesus or retrospected their concerns and modus operandi back to him, there is no earlier evidence recoverable. The later development of the narrative gospel, which in Mark is still essentially a passion narrative with an extended prologue of controversial incidents and miracle stories to affirm the divine—or at least God-certified—nature of the founder, reflected the need of an organized community or sect to authenticate itself by an appeal to historical events in the manner in which the Qumran Essenes (a group to which the Jerusalem group and other early settled churches of Palestine-Syria were probably similar in both organization and stance toward the rest of Judaism) produced the martyrology of the Teacher of Righteousness (Bennett and Edwards 1979, 238–42; Kee 1980, 94ff., 138–48; Käsemann 1982, 86–92; cf. Landay 1971, 249–62; Burrows 1958, 111–18, 355–62; Reicke 1964, xxxii–xxxvi; Freedman and Greenfield 1971; Wilson 1959, 55–76; cf. Pagels 1979, 102ff.).

From Q, then, and the oldest strands in Mark it would appear that Jesus functioned much in the manner of an Old Testament prophet, but with an especially strong element of the apocalyptic, millenarian expectation common at the time; his message focused upon ethical aphorisms, moral advice, parables, pronouncements of judgment, and calls for repentance—all in the face of the imminent, final coming of the reign of God (Perrin 1974, 288–300; Perrin 1976; Conzelmann 1973b; Bennett and Edwards 1979, 222–24, 238–43; Kee, Young, and Froehlich 1973, 422–23; Enslin 1956a, 157–68; Bultmann 1958; cf. Kee 1970 and 1980, 133–38; Jeremias 1972; Hengel 1981, 42, 66–67, 86–88). In this context even the healings—a basic part of the tradition but a phenomenon not unknown in ecstatic religions (Duling 1979, 18–22)—functioned primarily to authenticate Jesus' mission and to indicate that the Age of God was breaking into the world, while the final trip to Jerusalem after the essential failure of the Galilee mission may have been intended somehow to precipitate the final cosmic conflict.

A central feature of the teaching concerns that mysterious figure, the

Son of Man, who, building upon the account in Daniel where he is both the recipient of universal and eternal sovereignty at the *Eschaton* and also the personification of actual martyrs to the faith, is seen as the guarantor of God's coming righteous judgment. While it is uncertain that Jesus actually identified himself with the Son of Man, it would appear that for Jesus the Son of Man's acceptance of his audience would depend upon its having accepted Jesus' message (Bennett and Edwards 1979, 227–29; Küng 1976, 383; Nineham 1977, 44–47; Russell 1968, 127–42; cf. Tödt 1965; Higgins 1980). It is quite possible that Jesus saw himself in relation to the eschatological, heavenly Son of Man rather in the manner in which Christians are accustomed to see John the Baptist in relation to Jesus as Christ: that is, as the divinely ordained earthly forerunner. Such, at least, is the view of Bornkamm (1960, 172–76) and, essentially, of Wright and Fuller (1960, 281–85). Perrin (1974, 75–76; 1976, 160ff.) and Käsemann (1982, 37–44), on the other hand, doubt that the Son of Man concept had sufficient prominence in the pre-Christian period to have been seized upon as a metaphor by Jesus; they believe that all references to the Son of Man are the creations of the earliest church. All, however, agree that, on the one hand, Jesus did not claim accepted messianic titles or divine status and, on the other, that he did explicitly or by unmistakable implication claim an authority above any previous teacher in Jewish history—indeed, that he asserted for himself a final role as God's earthly agent completely unparalleled in the traditional religion. As Gager (1975, 29) notes, such opening up of new, alternative paths to the valued thing, new "redemptive media" controlled by the innovator(s) rather than by the establishment, is typical of millenarian cults.

Although the foregoing patterns appear appropriate to millenarian cults, it is the ethical teaching that enables us to identify the socioeconomic locus of the movement (cf. Gager 1975, 29). Küng (1976) and Theissen (1978) suggest that for Jesus the growing moral rigorism characteristic of Judaism in that era—which the Essenes met by withdrawing from the world into xenophobic and self-righteous isolation, and the Pharisees by developing an elaborate code of subsidiary regulations through which those who could make the effort might finesse the rigors of the Law without overtly abandoning the impossible ideal—was turned into a proclamation that all have sinned equally and are therefore equal in the sight of an absolutely holy but totally merciful God, and into a radical criticism of the establishment that claimed to enforce the moral code (cf. Braun 1979; Dodd 1970). To this was added an attitude of high respect for the ceremonial code as an institution but utter skepticism of the manner in which the ritual precepts and taboos, especially as these related to the Sabbath, ceremonial purity, and asceticism in general—features which supported the special status of the Sadducees and the urban wealthy among the Pharisees—were in fact carried out (cf. Duling 1979, 23–29; Rhein 1966, 80–94). A natural correlate was an acceptance of the "outsiders": demoniacs (presumably persons suffering from various forms of mental illness), moral failures (a category that would include many taboo breakers), others whose life circumstances violated the laws of ceremonial purity (for example, those suffering from certain illnesses), tax farmers (collaborationists), women (Jesus, probably, and the early church, certainly, held women in much higher regard than was the norm in Jewish or Greek society of the day), the poor, powerless, and downcast (without glorifying poverty or abandoning the criticism of the rich), and even the Gentiles (though often in the context of criticisms of the national leadership). The fact that the rich and powerful have more of the good things of life than the poor now forms part of a reversed evaluation that exalts the latter at the expense of the former (Hengel 1974a, 19, 26–34). Gager (1975, 24–25) points out that such reversals, and disputes over wealth in general, are a characteristic feature of modern millenarian movements.

The cultic or ritual aspects of the Jesus movement provide some support for this characterization. In this context, however, two interesting absences appear in the earliest tradition. The first is the lack of any concern with a Gentile mission. Although Gentiles as individuals are acceptable if they are on the scene, the concentration—as in the Hebrew prophetic tradition—is essentially on the response of the People of God, Israel, to God's plan. The second is the lack of any interest in baptism. This is odd (even though there could be no role for baptism as an initiation rite of a nonexistent church or as an admission ceremony for non-Jews when there was still no significant intention to secure followers from that source), since John's baptism had functioned as a rite of purification for the coming judgment. Evidently, the oldest traditions about Jesus reflect an early and noninstitutionalized stage in the growth of a millenarian movement, when attention was focused almost exclusively upon the preexisting religious (and political) community.

On the other hand, it does appear that the concept of the Messianic Banquet—to which all, including (or especially) the previously outcast, are invited—formed a central aspect of Jesus' preaching (Perrin 1976, 102–14). It is not improbable that a sacramental acting-out of this banquet, whether by Jesus himself or only later by his followers, lies behind the stories of the miraculous feedings. The accounts of the Last Supper, leaving aside the problems of its precise historicity and setting, reflect an especially significant example of this practice (Fuller 1963, 37, 57–58, 74, 102–4; Perrin 1974, 25–31, 45, 54, 77, 247; Nineham 1977). Moreover, it would appear that food taboos were the aspect of ritual law to which Jesus took special exception. Feeley-Harnik (1981) points out that in the Judaism of the time these taboos had come to bear a heavy weight of community identification and moral significance: hence the accusations of gluttony and drunkenness directed against Jesus (Perrin 1976, 119–22). This perhaps explains the strength of the hostility to Jesus among many leading citizens—that is, the urban upper-middle class—as well as the ruling elite. More significantly, in addition to being a particularly striking example of the introduction of alternative redemptive media, this ritual flouting of taboos that had become so central to the existing religious organization represented a strong rejection of the existing national leadership at all levels, even at the cost of deemphasizing or denying the accepted markers of national identity.

I would suggest that these values represented the view of the rural population, including their natural leaders on the local level among the craftsmen, small landholders, and petty entrepreneurs—the middling stratum of society and precisely the group from which Jesus and his more prominent disciples came (Bornkamm 1960, 151; Hengel 1974a, 16–28)—and that these values were directed not so much against the foreign overlords as against the local urban power structure centered in Jerusalem. The former were distant, almost a matter of background chatter, while the latter were an immediate day-to-day problem. The love ethic, then, which in fact was framed in the context of leaving just vengeance to the surely coming Lord, and the prominent theme that the present age was under demonic control may be seen as mechanisms by which social criticism could be maintained but also directed away from the local community and toward oppressive outsiders. In a very real sense one might say that Palestinian society was split in such a way that the national leadership had become the colonial oppressors of the rural population, much as in some Third World countries where the European-educated native rulers function as crypto-colonial masters, supported by a national army that is, in effect, an army of occupation (cf. Russell 1968, 27–37).

Such an interpretation explains the apparent rapid change of mood in Jerusalem between Palm Sunday and Good Friday. In reality, there was no change of mood: on Sunday Jesus was surrounded by a raucous crowd of antiestablishment pilgrims from the countryside; on Friday he found himself facing the urban population of Jerusalem, whose livelihood absolutely depended upon the Temple system (Theissen 1978, 55–57; Jeremias 1975, 21–27, 111–19). A further, even clearer, indication that Jerusalem represented the supremely dangerous place for would-be reformers of the Law is provided by the better-documented situation in the first two decades of the church. It seems that Peter was much more willing to deemphasize or ignore food taboos and regulations concerning Gentiles on those occasions when he was well away from Jerusalem. The need for Peter and other members of the Jerusalem church to walk warily in appearing to attack the Law and the Temple is probably the most reasonable explanation for Peter's seeming vacillation on these points that so irritated Paul (Reicke 1964, xvi–xx; Conzelmann 1973a, 109–12).

Jesus was, then, a radical, nativistic critic of an internal colonialism and received the treatment generally accorded such individuals. The months and years following the crucifixion presented the emerging church with many problems. The death of their leader was not, however, one of them. There is absolutely no doubt that the inner circle of those who experienced the "Easter event" were convinced that Jesus was not dead. The consensus of scholarly study of the resurrection narratives is that the earliest stage was the visionary experience of the glorified Christ (as recounted in Paul's account in I Corinthians and implied in the purportedly early sermons in Acts). The story of the empty tomb probably emerged next, partly as a logical consequence of resurrection and partly because the author of the earliest gospel, the one traditionally attributed to Mark, ended his account with an empty tomb for his own theological reasons (Perrin 1977; cf. Johnson 1972,

9–13, 261–64). Finally, the physical appearances of the resurrected Jesus were added under the influence of the belief among the Pharisees that at the *Eschaton* the bodies of the just would be reanimated. The appearances also served to stress the unique experience and hence authority of the founding apostles (Duling 1979, 33–38; Küng 1976, 342–84; Schillebeeckx 1979, 329–53; Marxsen 1970, 89–95; Pagels 1979, 5–27; Ruef 1977, xix–xxiii, 157–79; Fuller 1980). The Emmaus story and the discourses in the Fourth Gospel clearly indicate an influence from the developing eucharistic piety of the church (cf. Feeley-Harnik 1981). Whether the initial experience was purely subjective ("hallucination") or something more, as Christian orthodoxy has always maintained, makes no difference to the analysis (cf. Conzelmann 1973a, 33, 38–42). Groups experiencing the disappointment of fervent expectations have been known to see things that the outside observer would say were not there (Festinger, Riecken, and Schachter 1964). Whatever the opinions of nonbelievers, as Lowie (1963) has noted, vivid religious experience will move the believer to Herculean exertions.

A more serious discomfiture may have been the continued delay of the confidently awaited *Eschaton*—an expectation still central to Christian belief in the middle of the century (Whiteley 1969). Yet in the long run this had positive consequences. Festinger, Riecken, and Schachter (1964) point out that a common consequence of discomfiture is the missionary imperative, and Dodd (1964) has argued that the evidence provided by the Pauline epistles and by the apparently early traditional material in Acts shows that the first Christians very quickly began to preach Jesus, clearly identified as the Christ, as the divinely foretold, appointed, vindicated, and now heaven-situated agent of God's redemption (cf. Enslin 1956b, 171–74). Soon the disorders consequent upon a quarrel between the first Greek-speaking Jewish Christians at Jerusalem and certain strictly observant Hellenistic Jews led to a persecution that scattered these Christians throughout Palestine and Syria (Enslin 1956a, 178–79; Hengel 1983, 5–16). With continued delay the *Eschaton* becomes, as it were, increasingly stretched out, with the Son of Man—now seen as the *presently* active agent of God's redemption and of course fully identified with Jesus—reigning for the time being in the heavens, immediately under God. The result is the emergence of a cosmic locus of religious identification free of the limitations of place and nationality (Kee 1980, 47–48, 88–90).

This is the stage probably represented in the famous pre-Pauline hymn quoted in Philippians 2:6–11 (provided one understands that "the divine nature" or "image of God" meant being made in God's image like Adam [Houldon 1977, 67–84]). Although these developments had clearly been foreshadowed by Jesus' placement of religious purity on a footing other than that of the traditional ethnic boundary markers (Käsemann 1982, 101–2), Hengel (1983, 19, 23, 33–35, 58–63, 85–92) argues persuasively that it was in the earliest communities of Greek-speaking Jewish Christians—who began as a semidetached wing of the Jerusalem church but now shifted their center to Antioch, where "the disciples were called Christians first" (Acts 11:26b)—that this decisive step was taken. The same author suggests that this development of the original adoptionist (or, better, proclamationist: cf. Romans 1:3–4) Christology of the early church was in fact associated with the linguistic shift from Aramaic to Greek (Hengel 1983, 24–29). In addition, it was the Hellenistic Jewish Christians who began a major missionary effort toward the Gentile world (Conzelmann 1973a, 56–67).

The next step, possibly taken by Paul, was to follow the lead provided by those elements of Diaspora Judaism who had made the personified Wisdom of God the agent of creation and the guarantor of cosmic stability. This view shows obvious Platonic influence but may in fact have ultimately come from the Egyptian concept of Maat, goddess of truth and daughter of Ra, by way of those aberrant Egyptian Jews who maintained their own temple and worshiped subordinate deities alongside Yahweh (Duling 1979, 43–54; Kee 1980, 35–36; Landay 1971, 191–93; Stone 1973); in it, God's Wisdom becomes fully expressed on earth—incarnate, as it were—in the Mosaic Law as the divinely ordained mechanism of salvation. By another view, the Law was brought from God to man by angelic intermediaries, a concept that forms the background of the argument in the Epistle to the Hebrews (Buchanan 1972; cf. Conzelmann 1973a, 115, 136). The identification of the prophet Jesus with God's creative reason—the stage seen in the hymn of Colossians 1:15–20, whether composed by Paul or quoted from an earlier source (Houlden 1977, 134–43, 155–

73)—obviously shifts the balance still further from local to universal identity (Kee 1980, 106; Hengel 1983, 42–43; Meeks 1983, 108, 180–92; Wright and Fuller 1960, 304–6, 325ff.). Moreover, this development certainly tends to set faith in Jesus, now rapidly becoming the second person of the Trinity, in theological opposition to adherence to the Law, with its ethnic and national identity (Cornfeld and Freedman 1976, 303–5; Selby 1962, 152–61, 300–305).

Both conceptual transformations shift salvation from a concern with national and ethnic survival to the universal and fundamental problems of meaningful life and bearable death that were characteristic of the prosperous, multiethnic, rootless urban centers of the broader Mediterranean world (Edwards 1981; Meeks 1983, 92–94, 118–21, 157; Selby 1962, 312–22; Cornfeld and Freedman 1976, 286–87; cf. Hengel 1974a, 40–41). The naturalness, though perhaps not the inevitability, of this further shift is supported by recent detailed comparisons of the theology of the Pauline epistles with that of the purportedly early sermons in Acts, despite the later date of the latter work (and the problems of text and authorship associated with it), provided one assumes that the author of Acts either had very early sources to draw upon or was consciously attempting to reconstruct (and idealize) an earlier stage that he knew to have existed (Vielhauer 1980; Moule 1980; Schweizer 1980). Each change, however great its theological and sociological implications, is but a small incremental addition to the stage reached by previous adjustments. Moreover, most of them draw upon concepts available in the sectarian Judaism of the time.

Thus, although the view sometimes expressed that Paul and others made primitive Christianity into a Hellenistic missionary religion by abruptly imposing upon it a great cargo of exotic ideas imported from the Greco-Roman mystery cults is a misreading of the actual historical development, the fact is that Christianity now became highly attractive to the larger audience. There was, to be sure, some loss of distinctiveness. Of the four emerging messianic titles, "Son of Man" soon ceased to be intelligible in the new context. "Christ" (the translation of "messiah"—that is, "anointed"—a term traditionally applied to the king or any human agent of God's work) became a proper name. "Lord" (applied in the Old Testament indifferently to the king, to God, and to other luminaries) and "Son of God" (sometimes applied to the actual king as the divinely empowered ruler of God's people by an analogy with the son of an earthly sovereign) became identified with the various divine personages of pagan religions not notable for their concern with historical process or social justice (Bennett and Edwards 1979, 244; Edwards 1981; Kee, Young, and Froehlich 1973, 215–17). Yet the very Jewishness of the first missionaries and their custom of citing the Jewish scriptures in support of their messianic claims for Jesus—a practice extensively demonstrated in the speeches in Acts or in such works as Romans or Hebrews (Williams 1964, 36–48, 65–69, 75–80, 98–110; Dodd 1964; Buchanan 1972; Barrett 1957)—ensured that the teaching of the Old Testament prophets and theological historians would be maintained (Conzelmann 1973a, 43–52, 139–42).

There were also great advantages to the shift. Malherbe (1977) and Meeks (1983) point out that in addition to a certain number of the downtrodden, Christianity proved to be especially attractive to the upper artisan class and small businessman and -woman of the Hellenistic cities. These persons, often of moderate wealth or at least comfortably well off but also typically excluded from full participation in social, political, and cultic affairs, were precisely the socially transitional and status-inconsistent individuals who would be ripe for conversion to new routes to supernaturally based power and prestige. Moreover, such persons were accustomed to travel into many different settings in the course of their work (Malherbe 1977, 63–65, 75); they were in effect specialists in interethnic communication. Assuming the sixteenth chapter of Romans to be appropriately attached to that epistle, the large number of Christians in Rome known to Paul before his first arrival is most impressive. Suetonius tells us that before A.D. 50 there had been disorders in the Jewish community of Rome "under influence of Chrestus"—almost certainly a reference to early Christian preaching (Barrett 1957, 11–13, 280–87; Dunkerly 1957, 25–26; Conzelmann 1973a, 113–14, 130, 164–67). Because these persons were often above the average in intelligence, executive ability, and wealth, they could offer their houses as meeting places, a practice possibly patterned after the informal schools that already existed about Epicurean and Cynic philosophers. They could also support the travels of Christian missionaries. Malherbe notes that Paul's missionary "establishment" consisted of about forty persons who supported themselves or were maintained by donations of another several dozen (Malherbe 1977, 20–26, 41–48; cf. Edwards 1981; Hengel 1974a, 35–39, 49–

51, 61–65). These persons generally were favorable to and got along reasonably well with the Roman authorities—a fact which, along with simple prudence, probably explains Paul's markedly progovernment stance in the thirteenth chapter of Romans (Barrett 1957, 243–49).

It may well be that the evolving church did disappoint some of its poorer adherents. Concern over economic and political agitation among the membership almost certainly lies behind some of the preaching in the Catholic Epistles of the middle and latter part of the first century (Reicke 1964, xxii–xxix). The issue of the affordability of meat and other elite foods, a matter closely connected with the provision of animal flesh from the sacrifices at the city temples, certainly was a major factor in Paul's discussions of idolatry. The issue was also part of his efforts to shift the Christian Eucharist away from the free-form, often ecstatic, feast representative of the messianic banquet (indicated by the references in Acts, the possibly late-first-century and quite conservative church manual called the Didache, and perhaps the heavenly hymns of the fourth and fifth chapters of the Book of Revelation) to a more purely symbolic—even somber—memorial of the Last Supper and the Crucifixion. It was a change possibly influenced by contemporary commemorative feasts for the dead and one that shifted the focus of the rite for the rest of Christian history (Ruef 1977, xxiv–xxvii, 88–123; Barrett 1973; Staniforth 1968, 9–10, 225–26, 231–34; Sweet 1979, 114–26; cf. Meeks 1983, 157–60; Wright and Fuller 1960, 288–90, 311–12). The critical importance of this modification, not only in removing potentially disruptive class tensions from the central rite of Christianity (Meeks 1983, 69–71, 97–100; cf. Harris 1978, 177–79) but also in strengthening both the supernatural warranty of the community and the authority of the leaders who served as guarantors of the rite's institution (Käsemann 1982, 114, 121–22, 131–34), probably explains the large role played by early eucharistic practice in the formation of the gospel narratives and hence of a specifically Christian Bible itself (Bornkamm 1960, 160–62; Conzelmann 1973b, 82–85; and Fuller 1963, 101–4, among others; Jeremias 1977 argues for a much greater historicity to the accounts of the Last Supper).

The important point is that the antiestablishment views of the Hebrew prophets, although at times downplayed and kept in the background, were now in increasingly formalized and literary form coursing through the communication channels of the Roman empire—not unlike those clever viruses which, rather than damaging their host immediately after infection, enter the latter's genetic structure to be reproduced with the rest of that material and then, many reproductions later, actively infect all of the host's descendants. Moreover, the strength of this fortunate infection was such that subsequently these views could never be completely or permanently disallowed, not even by the institutional church itself on those (regrettably, all too frequent) later occasions when it in its turn became the servitor of the ruling class. Even then the tradition contained at its very core an irremovable, corrective, dissident countercurrent of great power. It is, to be sure, all too true that the new faith was not free of the exclusiveness and even dogmatism characteristic of many Iron Age missionary religions. As Theissen (1978, 118–19) points out, the church unfortunately did carry over—from the clash of parties in ancient Palestine and from its early struggles to survive—an element of narrow ethnocentrism and self-righteousness, reworked into an often bigoted, mean-spirited, and obscurantist role for the guardians of orthodoxy. Yet the ancient nativistic and peasant orientation of Yahwism, freed of its ties to a specific ethnicity by the activity of Jesus and his followers, ensured that however narrow-minded the new cult might at times be, one of its most enduring prejudices would be a bias (at least latent) in favor of those on the bottom of the social order. This created a situation in which society's core ideology stood in a relationship of creative tension with the rest of the social order, not only supporting it but recurringly subjecting it to judgment. These contentious and liberating ideals were, in other words, moving into position to play their central, long-lasting, and ultimately progressive role in the shaping of Western civilization. No matter how self-satisfied and "moral" society's leaders might claim to be, they could never escape the ongoing tradition of radical social criticism.

Civilization: Its Burdens and Its Blessings

MILES RICHARDSON AND MALCOLM C. WEBB

It seems to be certain that our present day civilization does not inspire in us a feeling of well-being.

—Sigmund Freud, *Civilization and Its Discontents,* n.d., 32

Today, as the paper-thin children of Ethiopia stare at us with eyes dulled to the point of death, Freud's critique in its mannered pace seems ironic, almost satirical. The great adventure that our ancestors launched some 6,000 years ago in the Old World and later, independently, in the New has become, in a way difficult to understand, a curse and self-imposed burden that we struggle to carry. The very creativity that in the past bespoke our unique knowledge and skill now, in the form of nuclear power, threatens us with instant annihilation and our children with an unlivable future. Today, we must confront that which we have created and examine both the thing itself and our views of it. Let us, then, review this volume's anthropological critique of civilization to underscore the contributions its authors have afforded us. As we do so, let us retain a sense of balance so that at the end, along with the burdens, we may also count our blessings.

In his valuable overview, Baer notes that anthropologists have always felt uncomfortable with civilization and that this ambivalence has crystalized into opposing prospective and retrospective assessments. On the one hand, dazzled by civilization's brilliance, we have praised its advances in technology and social structure; on the other, civilization's threat to the noncivilized has stirred our sense of justice, and since Morgan we have been quick both to search for and to defend the primitive. This defense became the cornerstone of the retrospective doctrine of cultural relativism, and cultural relativism in turn became the unconscious ethos in the folk culture of American anthropology. Yet paradoxically, in its pursuit of the aesthetic vision of cultural integration, Boasian cultural relativism all but ignored the role of civilization in creating the part cultures of "domestic dependents." The resurgence of cultural evolutionism brought this role to the forefront of anthropological scrutiny, and Leslie White, as Baer most tellingly observes, became an eloquent spokesman of the retrospective critique of civilization.

From Baer's summary, we move to particular studies of discontents. The first of these asks: What price civilization? In the context of the debate as to the presence of tuberculosis in the New World prior to Columbus, Blakely and Mathews consider the problem of distinguishing tuberculosis from other infectious diseases (such as blastomycosis) in skeletal populations. In so doing, the authors demonstrate the power of a truly comprehensive biocultural science. They not only establish a convincing argument for tuberculosis in the prehistoric South but also develop an epidemiological perspective that recognizes the coevolutionary relationship between predator and prey, between disease and culture. The independent occurrence of tuberculosis in the New World among agriculturalists on their way to civilization dramatically supports such a perspective. It also affirms that agriculture, once considered the hallmark of civilization's control over nature, levies a charge for its harvest.

The next study also examines the course of civilization in the aboriginal South, but its author concerns himself less with the evolution of indigenous culture than with its devolution. He asks: If prehistoric development in the South culminated in the Mississippian period of mound construction, then what caused that impressive development to end? What brought Paradise down? Drawing upon his intensive knowledge of the area, Peebles can find the cause neither in subsistence nor in disease. Instead, the collapse came down from the top: the elite, for whatever reason, were no longer able to substantiate their position through the distribution of socially valuable goods to the general populace, and as a consequence they lost their claim to tribute. Without that created demand, the extensive trade routes that flowed into Moundville dried up, and down came Paradise.

With the collapse of Paradise came social equality—at least, as Peebles points out, in death—and a precipitous decline in health. The arrival of the Spanish, then the French, and finally the English and the Goose Creek men energized the twisting spiral of social devolution. Fed by the trade in deerskins and Indian slaves, the devolution reached hurricane force, and out of its swirling, at the time of the American Revolution, spun the Five Civilized Tribes.

The vortices that sucked up deer and slaves across the South become, in the next chapter, embodied in actual tornadoes and floods. Wind and rain have always threatened human life, but their potential for disaster has increased, as the author documents, with the growth of the dense population centers associated with civilization. In his review of recent catastrophes, Greenamyre demonstrates that the increase in physical stress among larger numbers of people is accompanied by increased psychic stress. The severity of such mental disturbances—which include depression, anger, and guilt in amounts so detrimental as to render people incapable of seeking aid—is only now being recognized. Furthermore, the efforts to provide assistance are often hindered by the nature of the stress, which can mask itself behind a victim's seemingly compliant, obedient behavior, and by bureaucratic conflict between the relief agencies themselves, which may degenerate into squabbling as to who owns what disaster. The formation of adequate responses to disasters must rest, the author concludes, on the awareness of the evolutionary relationship among natural phenomena of earthquakes and floods, technological accidents, increasingly dense populations, and deepening psychic trauma.

The next chapter in the anthropological critique of civilization departs from a consideration of the more biological, physical qualities to attend to an attribute often selected as *the* criterion of civilization—literacy. Durbin recounts a program designed to enhance the appreciation of Mexico's indigenous linguistic heritage. Participants in the program achieved literacy in their own Mesoamerican languages, yet the native speakers seldom considered writing in their own language to be on a par with writing in Spanish. They either limited the writing of their home language to a ceremonial, dedicatory role or transcribed their speech patterns onto paper to produce not measured thought and stylistic elegance but simply written talk.

Using insights gained from this project, Durbin interprets our own indigenous attempt to become literate in English. In our linguistic history, runic writing, despite its capabilities, never advanced beyond a ceremonial, dedicatory role. As the Mesoamerican speaker cannot escape the burden of Spanish, so we could not shuck off the yoke of Latin. Indeed, only recently have we begun to choose two-fisted, four-letter Anglo-Saxon over the effeminate and floral Latin; even today, when we try to convey our cultural selves, we abandon barbaric "shit" for the more civilized "defecation."

"Celistino and His Discontents" gives us an account of a Nahuatl community not far from Mexico City, some of whose people have lost their indigenous language, and more have lost *el modo del indio,* the Indian way of life based on subsistence cultivation and community service. In exchange the people of Jonotla have found Spanish, capitalism, and an anthropologist. The account is all too familiar, but rarely has it been recited with the eloquent realism accorded it by Reck. The informant has a name, Celistino, and Celistino talks. Likewise, the anthropologist is an "I," who discovers that no longer can he hide behind a research design, but that he must confront, instead, what it is to be human. The confrontation shapes itself into a metalogue in which the characters not only speak but speak about the structure of their conversations. The metalogue, which by now includes the reader, extracts us out of the subjective world of everyday science, and transports us into the naked objectivity of self-reflection. Small wonder that in the fresh light of this new world we join Celistino and his friend Silvano, and laugh until we can laugh no more.

The theme of self-reflexivity and its attendant alienation continues into the next critique. In a carefully advanced argument, King presents the proposition that with an increase in the content of culture and the accompanying complexities in its organization—that is, with the emergence of civilization—the unique constellations of behavioral traits that constitute distinct personalities have increasingly diverged from one another. The more civilized we become, the more individualized we are. Like earlier forms, modern civilization relies on the past to formulate models of acceptable behavior for the future. Yet the very democracy of knowledge in the modern condition blurs the limits between acceptable behavior and the behavior that lies ahead in the unexplored realms of possibility, behavior defined at the moment as nonhuman and therefore evil. As the known world expands to include all culture and there is more to share, we share less; only during infancy and senility do we come together. With a consciousness that expands to the awareness of infinity, alienation from specific cultures becomes alienation from culture. We are thrown upon ourselves to become our own worlds, and what earlier was beyond the limits of social morality is that which we are.

An alternative to alienation, Guillotte suggests in the next essay, is our ability to switch logical fields. A logical field is a constellation of roles that we adopt, or invent perhaps, for ourselves so that the world appears at the moment to be eminently sound, and even sane. Conceptually, "logical field" appears similar to "situation" in the sense that if "men define the situations as real, they are real in their consequences" (Thomas and Thomas 1938, 572). Our ability both to commit ourselves totally to a position and then to disregard it happily when it no longer suits us Guillotte locates in the primate—indeed mammalian—propensity to play. Likewise, the ability to focus selectively on a stream of sounds makes language acquisition possible, and the same ability to redefine the meaning of particular sound streams permits the coherent expansion of language to cover new experience. Such a predisposition to reconstruct the world preadapts us for living, by and large comfortably, in the mass of contradictions that constitutes civilization. Politicians the world over are those most adept at such sleight-of-hand logic; others, the Serpicos and Herberts, are not so comfortable at redefining what once was truth into what is now merely inconvenient. They are the "uncivilized boors" who threaten the structure the rest of us have so carefully patched together.

Are not the boors kin to the cultural catatonics who, faced with the absurd logics of civilization, withdraw into the sanity of their private worlds? In turn, do not both boor and catatonic show a resemblance to the anthropologist, who seeks among the contradictions of alternate fields the secret that they hide?

In the final chapter of this critique, Webb joins a sophisticated appreciation of the cultural ecology of nativistic movements with an equally thorough reading of biblical scholarship to produce an interpretation of Christianity from (in the terms of the first chapter) a retrospective stance. Beginning with a delineation of the socioeconomic forces at work in Palestine, the author traces the transformation of the Jesus movement from an expression directed toward a single ethnic group's own colonial oppressors to the emergence of a multiethnic Christianity transcending time and place. Central to the transformation was the construction—out of the fate of a nativistic critic of internal colonialism: death by crucifixion—of a divinely foretold and heaven-situated agent of redemption. Accompanying the change from Jesus to Christ was the reduction of the ecstatic, messianic feast into the reenactment of the sacrificial crucifixion, the linguistic shift from Aramaic to Greek, and the expansion from a rural to an urban middle-class base. The transformation may have pacified a more direct call-to-arms confrontation with the powerful; at the same time the synthesis perpetuated, in a manner not easily ignored, the prophetic call for justice. Thus, utilizing the more basic elements of cultural ecology, Webb has built a view of Christianity not as an ideology functioning to keep the oppressed in line but as a voice, reverberating in the halls of the mighty, that lets the oppressed speak. And whenever those in power claim access to an absolute morality, the voice grows in force until it threatens to bring them down.

Having reviewed the chapters in this anthropological assessment of civilization, we may now assess the assessment. According to the authors, the burdens we imposed upon ourselves when we became civilized include disease, genocide, physical disaster, linguistic ambivalence, alienation, and hypocrisy—quite a cargo for a bipedal primate. Mixed with that cargo, however, are blessings, and the blessings make it possible for such frail creatures as we to shoulder our responsibilities. The blessings include the subduing, if not the taming, of tuberculosis; creative responses to both cultural and physical tornadoes in the shape of the Five Civilized Tribes and in the form of sensitive programs of crisis intervention; and the ability, through the alternation of logical fields, to live together in diversity. These are important blessings, and our step is made lighter because of them; still others of equal significance await counting. Principal among them is the often-considered criterion of civilization: writing.

Writing is more than a tool that allowed the priest of ancient Babylon to record the talents of wheat brought to the temple. With writing the priest could turn the interior voices in his head into external narrative, so that the gods might speak not only to him in the secret recesses of the temple but to all readers everywhere. Writing permits the construction of a world apart from the immediacy of oral conversation, a world that takes leave of its creator, a world that even transcends death, so that today we may read the mind of the priest and in so doing re-create him as we re-create Jesus when we read the Bible, what Christians call the Word, the Holy Word—that is, the written word.

When we write, we can read what we thought; writing separates us from our ideas, and so with writing we achieve a self-reflexivity which, in its intense clarity, is unlike other reflections in ritual, painting, or even television. Thus, with writing, the author also changes. The priest listening to the gods becomes the anthropologist listening to the people.

With writing, the anthropologist is able to do more than count the *fanegas* of maize traded at the market. With writing, the anthropologist can objectify the conversations of the people about him so that they may speak to distant audiences about their accomplishments, about their worries, about their dreams. He can become their myth-teller.

The blessing of writing can, as Durbin wrote, be a burden, or worse, as Reck (and Gatewood 1984) noted, a cop-out. When the anthropologist allows himself to be seduced by writing's objectivity, he forsakes the experiential, the world of flesh and bone (Unamuno 1972), the habitat of us bipedal primates, and becomes lost in the passive voice of selfless prose. Even the *fanegas* of maize, shucked under a hot sun, shelled in the cool patio, and loaded on battered trucks that hurl brakeless down narrow roads to the early morning market disappear into neat rows of bloodless figures.

The blessing that writing bestows upon us, objective reflexivity, must be claimed if we are to document the march from African savanna to lunar base and consider its meaning. To accomplish the task, we need the perspective of this critique, a perspective that is truly anthropological, critical of, yet sympathetic to, the human endeavor. From this perspective, we anthropologists stand together in laughter—not in the bitter voice of despair but in the wonderful sound of a species celebrating in writing the trajectory of its peculiar destiny.

References

Adler, Alexandra. 1943. Neuropsychiatric Complications in Victims of Boston's Cocoanut Grove Disaster. *Journal of the American Medical Association* 123:1098–1101.

Allison, M. J., D. Mendoza, and A. Pezzia. 1973. Documentation of a Case of Tuberculosis in Pre-Columbian America. *American Review of Respiratory Diseases* 107:985–91.

Anderson, B. W. 1975. *Understanding the Old Testament,* 3rd ed. Englewood Cliffs, N.J.: Prentice-Hall.

Arendt, Hannah. 1969. *The Human Condition.* Chicago: University of Chicago Press.

Bareis, Charles J., and James W. Porter, eds. 1984. *American Bottom Archaeology.* Urbana: University of Illinois Press.

Barrett, C. K. 1957. *A Commentary on the Epistle to the Romans.* New York: Harper & Row.

______. 1973. *A Commentary on the Second Epistle to the Corinthians.* New York: Harper & Row.

Bateson, Gregory. 1972. *Steps to an Ecology of Mind.* New York: Ballantine Books.

Bellah, Robert N. 1965. Religious Evolution. In *Reader in Comparative Religion: An Anthropological Approach,* 2nd ed., ed. William A. Lessa and Evon Z. Vogt, 73–87. New York: Harper & Row.

Bennett, R. A., and O. C. Edwards. 1979. *The Bible for Today's Church.* New York: Seabury Press.

Birch, Walter de Gray. 1887. *Cartularium Saxonicum,* vols. 1–3. London: Whithing.

Black, Thomas K., III. 1979. *The Biological and Social Analyses of a Mississippian Cemetery from Southeast Missouri.* Anthropological Papers of the Museum of Anthropology, University of Michigan, No. 68. Ann Arbor: University of Michigan Press.

Blaufarb, Herbert, and Jules Levine. 1972. Crisis Intervention in an Earthquake. *Social Work* 17(4):16–19.

Boas, Franz. 1928. *Anthropology in Modern Life*. New York: Norton.
______. 1938. *The Mind of Primitive Man*, rev. ed. New York: Macmillan.
Bodley, John H. 1976. *Anthropology and Contemporary Human Problems*. Menlo Park, Calif.: Cummings.
Bornkamm, G. 1960. *Jesus of Nazareth*. New York: Harper & Row.
Boyd, Mark F., Hale G. Smith, and John W. Griffin. 1951. *Here They Once Stood*. Gainesville: University of Florida Press.
Bozeman, Tandy K. 1981. Moundville Phase Sites in the Black Warrior Valley, Alabama: Preliminary Results of the UMMA Survey. *Southeastern Archaeological Conference Bulletin* 24:84–86.
______. 1982. Moundville Phase Communities in the Black Warrior River Valley, Alabama. Ph.D. dissertation, University of California, Santa Barbara.
Braidwood, R. J. 1964. *Prehistoric Men*. Glenview, Ill.: Scott, Foresman.
Braun, H. 1979. *Jesus of Nazareth: The Man and His Times*. Philadelphia: Fortress Press.
Bright, J. 1972. *A History of Israel*. Philadelphia: Westminster Press.
Brown, James A., ed. 1971. *Approaches to the Social Dimensions of Mortuary Practices*. Society for American Archaeology Memoir 25. Washington: Society for American Archaeology.
______. 1975. The Impact of European Presence on Indian Culture. In *Conquest for Empire 1500–1775*, ed. John B. Elliott, 6–24. Indianapolis: Indiana Historical Society.
Brown, Phillip M. 1975. Early Indian Trade in the Development of South Carolina. *South Carolina Historical Magazine* 76:118–28.
Buchanan, G. W. 1972. *To the Hebrews: Translation, Comment and Conclusions*. Anchor Bible, vol. 36. Garden City, N.Y.: Doubleday.
Buikstra, J. E. 1976a. Differential Diagnosis: An Epidemiological Model. *Yearbook of Physical Anthropology* 20:316–28.
______. 1976b. The Caribou Eskimo: General and Specific Disease. *American Journal of Physical Anthropology* 45:351–68.
______, ed. 1981. *Prehistoric Tuberculosis in the Americas*. Evanston, Ill.: Northwestern University Archaeological Program.
Buikstra, J. E., and D. C. Cook. 1980. Paleopathology: An American Account. *Annual Review of Anthropology* 9:433–70.
Bultmann, R. 1951–1955. *Theology of the New Testament*. New York: Scribner.
______. 1958. *Jesus Christ and Mythology*. New York: Scribner.
______. 1968. *The History of the Synoptic Tradition*. New York: Harper & Row.
______. 1980. *Primitive Christianity in Its Contemporary Setting*. Philadelphia: Fortress Press.

Burrows, M. 1958. *More Light on the Dead Sea Scrolls.* New York: Viking.

Carlton, Charles. 1970. *Descriptive Syntax of the Old English Charters.* The Hague: Mouton.

Carneiro, Robert L. 1981a. Leslie A. White. In *Totems and Teachers: Perspectives on the History of Anthropology,* ed. Sydel Silverman, 209–51. New York: Columbia University Press.

———. 1981b. The Chiefdom, Precursor of the State. In *The Transition to Statehood in the New World,* ed. Grant D. Jones and Robert R. Kautz, 37–75. Cambridge University Press.

Cartwright, Frederick F., with Michael D. Biddis. 1972. *Disease and History.* New York: Crowell.

Caudill, Harry M. 1972. Buffalo Creek Aftermath. *Saturday Review,* 26 August, 16–17.

Chard, Chester S. 1969. *Man in Prehistory.* New York: McGraw-Hill.

Chick, E. W., W. D. Sutliff, J. H. Rakich, and M. L. Furcolow. 1956. Epidemiological Aspects of Cases of Blastomycosis Admitted to Memphis, Tennessee Hospitals during the Period 1922–1954: A Review of 86 Cases. *American Journal of Medical Science* 231:253–62.

Childe, V. Gordon. 1950. The Urban Revolution. *Town Planning Review* 21:3–17.

Church, June S. 1974. The Buffalo Creek Disaster: Extent and Range of Emotional and/or Behavioral Problems. *Omega* 5:61–63.

Cleveland, M. 1940. Treatment of Tuberculosis of the Spine. *Journal of Bone and Joint Surgery* 22:824–39.

Colby, Benjamin. 1973. Comment on Paul Bohannan, Rethinking Culture: A Project for Current Anthropologists. *Current Anthropology* 14:366.

Coleman, James C. 1976. *Abnormal Psychology and Modern Life,* 5th ed. Glenview, Ill.: Scott, Foresman.

Comaroff, John L., and Simon Roberts. 1981. *Rules and Process: The Cultural Logic of Dispute in an African Context.* Chicago: University of Chicago Press.

Conzelmann, H. 1973a. *History of Primitive Christianity.* Nashville, Tenn.: Abingdon Press.

———. 1973b. *Jesus.* Philadelphia: Fortress Press.

Cornfeld, G., and D. N. Freedman. 1976. *Archaeology of the Bible: Book by Book.* New York: Harper & Row.

Count, Earl W. 1967. The Lactation Complex: A Phylogenetic Consideration of the Mammalian Mother/Offspring Symbiosis, with Special Reference to Man. *Homo* 18:38–54.

———. 1973. *Being and Becoming Human: Essays on the Biogram.* New York: Van Nostrand. (Originally published as *Das Biogram: Anthropologische Studien* [Frankfurt, 1970]).

Cowgill, George L. 1964. The End of Classic Maya Culture: A Review of Recent Evidence. *Southwestern Journal of Anthropology* 20:145–59.

Crane, Verner W. 1929. *The Southern Frontier.* Ann Arbor: University of Michigan Press.

Crumrine, N. Ross, and Lynne S. Crumrine. 1969. Where Mayos Meet Mestizos: A Model for the Social Structure of Culture Contact. *Human Organization* 28:50–57.

Cullmann, O. 1970. *Jesus and the Revolutionaries.* New York: Harper & Row.

Curren, Cailup B. 1982. The Alabama River Phase: A Review. In *Archaeology in Southwest Alabama: A Collection of Papers,* ed. Cailup B. Curren, 103–14. Camden, Ala.: Alabama Tombigbee Regional Commission.

Curren, Cailup B., and Keith J. Little. 1981. Archaeological Investigations (1933–1980) of the Protohistoric Period of Central Alabama. Unpublished manuscript, University of Alabama, Alabama Museum of Natural History.

Curren, Cailup B., Keith J. Little, and George E. Lankford. 1981. The Route of the Expedition of Hernando De Soto into Alabama. Paper presented at the 38th Annual Meeting of the Southeastern Archaeological Conference.

———. 1982. Archaeological Research Concerning 16th Century Spanish and Indians in Alabama. Unpublished report to Alabama Tombigbee Regional Commission.

Cushman, Henry B. 1899. *History of the Choctaw, Chickasaw, and Natchez Indians.* Greenville, Tex.: by the author.

Debo, Angie. 1934. *The Rise and Fall of the Choctaw Republic.* Norman: University of Oklahoma Press.

Decamp, David. 1974. Introduction: The Study of Pidgin and Creole Languages. In *Pidginization and Creolization of Language,* ed. Dell Hymes, 13–39. London: Cambridge University Press.

De la Fuente, Julio. 1967. Ethnic Relations. In *Handbook of Middle American Indians,* vol. 6, *Social Anthropology,* ed. M. Nash. Austin: University of Texas Press.

Demerath, Nicholas J., and Anthony F. C. Wallace, eds. 1957. *Human Organization* 16(2), special issue.

Dentan, Robert Knox. 1968. *The Semai: A Nonviolent People of Malaya.* New York: Holt, Rinehart & Winston.

DeRosier, Arthur H., Jr. 1970. *The Removal of the Choctaw Indians.* Knoxville: University of Tennessee Press.

Diamond, Stanley. 1964. A Revolutionary Discipline. *Current Anthropology* 5:432–36.

———. 1974. *In Search of the Primitive: A Critique of Civilization.* New Brunswick, N.J.: Transaction Books.

Diamond, Stanley, Bob Scholte, and Eric Wolf. 1975. Anti-Kaplan: Defining the Marxist Tradition. *American Anthropologist* 77:870–76.

Dodd, C. H. 1964. *The Apostolic Preaching and Its Developments.* New York: Harper & Row.

______. 1970. *The Founder of Christianity.* New York: Macmillan.

Douglas, Mary, and Baron Isherwood. 1978. *A World of Goods.* London: Penguin.

Drabek, Thomas E., and John S. Stephenson III. 1971. When Disaster Strikes. *Journal of Applied Social Psychology* 1:187–203.

Dubos, R., and J. Dubos. 1952. *The White Plague.* Boston: Little, Brown.

Duling, D. C. 1979. *Jesus Christ through History.* New York: Harcourt Brace Jovanovich.

Dunkerly, R. 1957. *Beyond the Gospels.* Harmondsworth: Penguin Books.

Earle, Timothy K. 1978. *Economic and Social Organization of a Complex Chiefdom: The Halelea District, Kauai, Hawaii.* Anthropological Papers of the Museum of Anthropology, University of Michigan, No. 63. Ann Arbor: University of Michigan Press.

Edwards, O. C. 1981. The New Testament Church: From Jesus to the Apologists. In *A Faithful Church: Issues in the History of Catechesis,* ed. J. H. Westerhoff III and O. C. Edwards, Jr., 10–48. Wilton, Conn.: Morehouse Barlow.

Eliade, Mircea. 1961. *The Sacred and the Profane: The Nature of Religion.* New York: Harper.

Enslin, M. S. 1956a. *Christian Beginnings,* Parts I, II. New York: Harper & Row.

______. 1956b. *Christian Beginnings,* Part III: *The Literature of the Christian Movement.* New York: Harper & Row.

Fagan, Brian M. 1983. *People of the Earth,* 4th ed. Boston: Little, Brown.

Feeley-Harnik, G. 1981. *The Lord's Table: Eucharist and Passover in Early Christianity.* Philadelphia: University of Pennsylvania Press.

Festinger, H., H. W. Riecken, and S. Schachter. 1964. *When Prophecy Fails: A Social and Psychological Study of a Modern Group That Predicted the Destruction of the World.* New York: Harper & Row.

Firey, Walter. 1967. Conditions for the Realization of Values Remote in Time. In *Sociological Theory, Values, and Sociocultural Change,* ed. Edward A. Tiryakian, 147–59. New York: Harper Torchbooks.

Fischer, John L. 1973. The Individual as the Crucial Locus of Culture. In *Socialization and Communication in Primary Groups,* ed. Thomas R. Williams, 439–48. The Hague: Mouton.

Fowler, Melvin L. 1974. *Cahokia, Ancient Capital of the Midwest.* New York: Addison-Wesley.

Frankenstein, Susan M., and Michael J. Rowlands. 1978. The Internal Structure and Regional Context of Early Iron Age Society in South-Western Germany. *Institute of Archaeology Bulletin* [London] 15:73–112.

Freedman, D. N., and J. C. Greenfield, eds. 1971. *New Directions in Biblical Archaeology.* Garden City, N.Y.: Doubleday.

Freud, Sigmund. 1962. *Civilization and Its Discontents,* trans. and ed. James Strachey. New York: Norton.

______. N.d. *Civilization and Its Discontents.* Garden City, N.Y.: Anchor Books.

Friedman, Jonathan. 1979. *Structure, System, and Contradiction.* Copenhagen: Nutuna Museum.

______. 1982. Catastrophe and Continuity in Social Evolution. In *Theory and Explanation in Archaeology,* ed. Colin Renfrew, Michael Rowlands, and B. Abbot Segraves, 175–96. New York: Academic Press.

Friedman, Jonathan, and Michael J. Rowlands, eds. 1977. *The Evolution of Social Systems.* London: Duckworth.

Fritz, Charles E. 1957. Disasters Compared in Six American Communities. *Human Organization* 16(2):6–9.

Fuller, R. H. 1963. *Interpreting the Miracles.* London: SCM Press.

______. 1980. *The Formation of the Resurrection Narratives.* Philadelphia: Fortress Press.

Furcolow, M. L., A. Balows, R. W. Menges, D. Pickar, J. T. McClellan, and A. Saliba. 1966. Blastomycosis. *Journal of the American Medical Association* 198:529–32.

Gager, J. G. 1975. *Kingdom and Community: The Social World of Early Christianity.* Englewood Cliffs, N.J.: Prentice-Hall.

Galloway, Patricia. 1981. Multidimensional Scaling for Mapping Ethnohistorical Narratives: Choctaw Villages in the Eighteenth Century. Paper presented at the Tenth Congress of the International Union of Pre- and Protohistoric Sciences.

Gatewood, John B. 1984. A Short Typology of Ethnographic Genres, or Ways to Write about Other People. *Anthropology and Humanism Quarterly* 4:5–10.

Gearing, Frederick O. 1974. The Structural Poses of 18th Century Cherokee Villages. In *Man In Adaptation: The Cultural Present,* ed. Yehudi A. Cohen, 181–87. Chicago: Aldine.

German, Daniel B., and Gregory G. Reck. 1978. The Hidden Application: The Method Is the Message. *Anthropology and Humanism Quarterly* 3:5–16.

Gillin, John. 1945. Parallel Cultures and the Inhibitions to Acculturation in a Guatemalan Community. *Social Forces* 24:1–14.

Gilman, Antonio. 1981. Social Stratification in Bronze Age Europe. *Current Anthropology* 22:1–23.
Gleser, Goldine C., Bonnie L. Green, and Carolyn Winget. 1981. *Prolonged Psychosocial Effects of Disaster.* New York: Academic Press.
Goldsmith, William, and Maurice Zeitlin. N.d. Don Quixote and Dr. Caplan. Unpublished paper.
Gough, Kathleen. 1968. New Proposals for Anthropologists. *Current Anthropology* 9:403–7.
Gouldner, Alvin W. 1970. *The Coming Crisis of Western Sociology.* New York: Avon Books.
Grant, F.C. 1957. *The Gospels: Their Origin and Growth.* New York: Harper.
Greenamyre, Edward L. 1980. The Role of the Anthropologist in Civil Emergency Preparedness Planning. *Practicing Anthropology* 2(6):14, 21–22.
Greenberg, James B. 1981. *Santiago's Sword: Chatino Peasant Religion and Economics.* Berkeley: University of California Press.
Griffin, James B. 1967. Eastern North American Archaeology: A Summary. *Science* 156:175–91.
Haddy, Alice, and Albert Hanson. 1981. Relative Dating of Moundville Burials. *Southeastern Archaeological Conference Bulletin* 24:97–99.
Hall, Robert L. 1975. Some Problems of Identity and Process in Cahokia Archaeology. Unpublished manuscript.
———. 1980. An Interpretation of the Two-Climax Model of Illinois Prehistory. In *Early Native Americans,* ed. David L. Browman, 401–62. The Hague: Mouton.
Hardin, Margaret Ann. 1981. The Identification of Individual Style in Moundville Engraved Vessels: A Preliminary Note. *Southeastern Archaeological Conference Bulletin* 24:108–10.
Harris, Marvin. 1968. *The Rise of Anthropological Theory.* New York: Crowell.
———. 1975. *Cows, Pigs, Wars and Witches: The Riddles of Culture.* New York: Vintage Books.
———. 1978. *Cannibals and Kings: The Origins of Culture.* New York: Vintage Books.
Harshbarger, Dwight. 1974. Picking Up the Pieces: Disaster Intervention and Human Ecology. *Omega* 5:55–59.
Haugen, Einer. 1976. *The Scandinavian Languages.* Cambridge, Mass.: Harvard University Press.
Helms, Mary W. 1979. *Ancient Panama: Chiefs in Search of Power.* Austin: University of Texas Press.
Hengel, M. 1971. *Was Jesus a Revolutionist?* Facet Books, Biblical Series, No. 28. Philadelphia: Fortress Press.

———. 1974a. *Property and Riches in the Early Church: Aspects of a Social History of Early Christianity.* Philadelphia: Fortress Press.

———. 1974b. *Judaism and Hellenism: Studies in Their Encounter in Palestine during the Early Hellenistic Period,* 2 vols. Philadelphia: Fortress Press.

———. 1977. *Crucifixion in the Ancient World and the Folly of the Message of the Cross.* Philadelphia: Fortress Press.

———. 1980. *Jew, Greeks and Barbarians: Aspects of the Hellenization of Judaism in the Pre-Christian Period.* Philadelphia: Fortress Press.

———. 1981. *The Charismatic Leader and His Followers.* New York: Crossroad.

———. 1983. *Between Jesus and Paul: Studies in the Earliest History of Christianity.* Philadelphia: Fortress Press.

Herbert, Anthony B., with James T. Wooten. 1973. *Soldier.* New York: Dell.

Higgins, A. J. B. 1980. *The Son of Man in the Teaching of Jesus.* Society for New Testament Studies, Monograph Series, No. 39. New York: Cambridge University Press.

Hill, Mary Cassandra. 1979. The Alabama River Phase: A Biological Synthesis and Interpretation. M.A. thesis, University of Tennessee, Knoxville.

Hockett, Charles F., and Robert Ascher. 1968. The Human Revolution. In *Readings in Anthropology,* 2nd ed., ed. Morton H. Freid, 1:323–46. New York: Crowell.

Hoebel, E. Adamson. 1966. *Anthropology: The Study of Man.* New York: McGraw-Hill.

———. 1972. *Anthropology: The Study of Man,* 4th ed. New York: McGraw-Hill.

Hooton, E. A. 1930. *The Indians of Pecos Pueblo.* New Haven, Conn.: Yale University Press.

Houlden, J. L. 1977. *Paul's Letters from Prison: Philippians, Colossians, Philemon and Ephesians.* Philadelphia: Westminster Press.

Howells, W. W., et al. 1940. *The Maya and Their Neighbors.* New York: Appleton-Century.

Hrdlicka, A. 1909. Tuberculosis among Certain Indian Tribes. In *Bureau of American Ethnology Bulletin 42.* Washington, D.C.: Government Printing Office.

Hsu, Francis L. K. 1961. American Core Value and National Character. In *Psychological Anthropology,* ed. Francis L. K. Hsu, 209–30. Homewood, Ill.: Dorsey Press.

Hudson, Charles. 1976. *The Southeastern Indians.* Knoxville: University of Tennessee Press.

Hudson, Charles, Marvin T. Smith, and Chester B. DePratter. 1984. The

Hernando De Soto Expedition: From Apalachee to Chiaha. *Southeastern Archaeology* 3(1):65–77.

Hymes, Dell. 1974. Preface. In *Pidginization and Creolization of Languages,* ed. Dell Hymes, 3–11. London: Cambridge University Press.

Jenkins, Ned J., and Jerry Nielsen. 1974. Archaeological Salvage Investigations at the West Jefferson Steam Plant Site, Jefferson County, Alabama. Unpublished report to Alabama Power Company.

Jeremias, J. 1972. *The Parables of Jesus,* rev. ed. New York: Scribner.

______. 1975. *Jerusalem in the Time of Jesus: An Investigation into Economic and Social Conditions during the New Testament Period.* Philadelphia: Fortress Press.

______. 1977. *The Eucharistic Words of Jesus.* Philadelphia: Fortress Press.

Johnson, Gregory A. 1982. Organizational Structure and Scalar Stress. In *Theory and Explanation in Archaeology,* ed. Colin Renfrew, Michael J. Rowlands, and B. Abbot Segraves, 389–421. New York: Academic Press.

Johnson, S. E. 1972. *A Commentary on the Gospel According to St. Mark.* London: Adam and Charles Black.

Jorgensen, Joseph G., with Shelton H. Davis and Robert O. Mathews. 1978. Energy, Agriculture and Social Science in the American West. In *Native Americans and Energy Development,* ed. Joseph G. Jorgensen et al., 3–16. Cambridge, Mass.: Anthropology Resource Center.

Käsemann, E. 1982. *Essays on New Testament Themes.* Philadelphia: Fortress Press.

Kastembaum, Robert. 1974. Disaster, Death and Human Ecology. *Omega* 5:65–72.

Keck, L. E. 1979. *Paul and His Letters.* Philadelphia: Fortress Press.

Kee, H. C. 1970. *Jesus in History: An Approach to Study of the Gospels.* New York: Harcourt, Brace & World.

______. 1980. *Christian Origins in Sociological Perspective: Methods and Resources.* Philadelphia: Westminster Press.

Kee, H. C., F. W. Young, and K. Froehlich. 1973. *Understanding the New Testament.* Englewood Cliffs, N.J.: Prentice-Hall.

Kerns, Robert D. 1976. Personal Communication from Associate Director of the Division of Professional Services, West Virginia Department of Mental Health, 21 May.

Kinston, Warren, and Rachel Rosser. 1974. Disaster: Effects on Mental and Physical State. *Journal of Psychosomatic Research* 18:437–56.

Krader, Lawrence. 1976. *Dialectic of Civil Society.* Assen/Amsterdam: Van Gorcum.

Kroeber, Alfred L. 1917. The Superorganic. *American Anthropologist* 19:41–54.

———. 1948. *Anthropology.* New York: Harcourt, Brace.
———. 1962. *A Roster of Civilizations.* Chicago: Aldine.
———. 1963. *An Anthropologist Looks at History.* Berkeley: University of California Press.
Kroes, William H. 1976. *Society's Victim—the Policeman: An Analysis of Job Stress in Policing.* Springfield, Ill.: Thomas.
Kundsin, K. 1962. Primitive Christianity in the Light of Gospel Research. In *Form Criticism: Two Essays on New Testament Research,* ed. R. Bultmann and K. Kundsin, 79–161. New York: Harper.
Küng, H. 1976. *On Being a Christian.* Garden City, N.Y.: Doubleday.
Lace, O. J. 1965. The Historical Background of New Testament Times. In *Understanding the New Testament,* ed. O. J. Lace, 11–63. Cambridge: Cambridge University Press.
Landay, J. M. 1971. *Silent Cities, Sacred Stones: Archaeological Discoveries in Israel.* New York: McCall Books.
Lanternari, V. 1963. *The Religions of the Oppressed: A Study of Modern Messianic Cults.* New York: Mentor Books.
Larsen, C. S. 1982. *The Anthropology of St. Catherines Island,* 3: *Prehistoric Human Biological Adaptation.* Anthropological Papers, vol. 57, pt. 3. New York: American Museum of Natural History.
Lauber, Almon Wheeler. 1913. *Indian Slavery in Colonial Times within the Present Limits of the United States.* Studies in History, Economics, and Public Law, vol. 54, no. 3. New York: Columbia University.
LeMay, M. 1975. The Language Capability of Neanderthal Man. *American Journal of Physical Anthropology* 43:9–14.
Lévi-Strauss, Claude. 1955. *Tristes Triopique.* Paris: Librairie Plon.
———. 1971. *Mythologiques,* IV: *L'homme nu.* Paris: Librairie Plon.
Lifton, Robert Jay. 1967. *Death in Life: Survivors of Hiroshima.* New York: Random House.
Lindermann, Eric. 1944. Symptomatology and Management of Acute Grief. *American Journal of Psychiatry* 101:141–48.
Lowie, R. H. 1963. Religion in Human Life. *American Anthropologist* 65:532–42.
Luther, Edward T. 1977. *Our Restless Earth: The Geologic Regions of Tennessee.* Knoxville: University of Tennessee Press.
Maas, Peter. 1973. *Serpico.* New York: Viking Press.
McKenzie, J. L. 1966. *The World of the Judges.* Englewood Cliffs, N.J.: Prentice-Hall.
McNeill, William H. 1976. *Plagues and People.* New York: Anchor Press/Doubleday.
Madsen, William, and Claudia Madsen. 1974. The Cultural Structure of Mex-

ican Drinking Behavior. In *Contemporary Cultures and Societies of Latin America,* ed. D. B. Heath. New York: Random House.

Malherbe, A. J. 1977. *Social Aspects of Early Christianity.* Baton Rouge: Louisiana State University Press.

Marx, Karl. 1959. Theses on Feuerbach. In *Marx and Engels: Basic Writings on Politics and Philosophy,* ed. Lewis S. Feuer, 243–45. Garden City, N.Y.: Doubleday Anchor.

Marxsen, W. 1970. *The Resurrection of Jesus of Nazareth.* Philadelphia: Fortress Press.

Meadows, Donnella H., et al. 1972. *The Limits to Growth.* New York: New American Library.

Meeks, W. A. 1983. *The First Urban Christians: The Social World of the Apostle Paul.* New Haven, Conn.: Yale University Press.

Mendenhall, G. E. 1973. *The Tenth Generation: The Origins of the Biblical Tradition.* Baltimore, Md.: Johns Hopkins University Press.

Michals, Lauren. 1981. The Exploitation of Fauna during the Moundville I Phase at Moundville. *Southeastern Archaeological Conference Bulletin* 24:91–93.

Milner, George R. 1981. Epidemic Disease in the Postcontact Southeast: A Reappraisal. *Mid-Continental Journal of Archaeology* 5(1):39–56.

Mooney, J. [1896] 1967. *The Ghost-Dance Religion and the Sioux Outbreak of 1890,* ed. Anthony F. C. Wallace. Chicago: University of Chicago Press.

Morgan, Lewis H. 1964. *Ancient Society,* ed. Leslie A. White. Cambridge, Mass.: Harvard University Press.

Morse, D. 1969. *Ancient Disease in the Midwest.* Report of Investigations, No. 15. Springfield: Illinois State Museum.

Morse, D., D. R. Brothwell, and P. J. Ucko. 1964. Tuberculosis in Ancient Egypt. *American Review of Respiratory Diseases* 90:524–41.

Moule, C. F. D. 1965. How the New Testament Came into Being. In *Understanding the New Testament,* ed. O. J. Lace, 64–120. Cambridge: Cambridge University Press.

———. 1980. The Christology of Acts. In *Studies in Luke-Acts,* ed. L. E. Keck and J. L. Martyn, 159–85. Philadelphia: Fortress Press.

———. 1982. *The Birth of the New Testament,* 3rd ed. New York: Harper & Row.

Nader, Laura. 1972. Up the Anthropologist—Perspectives Gained from Studying Up. In *Reinventing Anthropology,* ed. Dell Hymes, 284–311. New York: Vintage Books.

Needham, Rodney. 1978. *Primordial Characters.* Charlottesville: University of Virginia Press.

Neill, S. 1966. *The Interpretation of the New Testament, 1861–1961.* London: Oxford University Press.

Nineham, D. E. 1977. *Saint Mark.* Philadelphia: Westminster Press.

Ohio State University Disaster Research Center. 1975a. Delivery of Mental Health Services in the Xenia Disaster (preliminary report). O.S.U. Disaster Research Center.

———. 1975b. Interim Survey Report (preliminary report). O.S.U. Disaster Research Center.

———. N.d. Some Implications of the Study, VII. O.S.U. Disaster Research Center.

Ophuls, William. 1974. The Scarcity Society. *Harper's* 246:47–52.

Orr, William F., and Stephen C. Cappanari. 1964. The Emergence of Language. *American Anthropologist* 66:318–24.

Pagels, E. 1979. *The Gnostic Gospels.* New York: Random House.

Payne, Claudine. 1982. Farmsteads and Districts: A Model of Fort Walton Settlement Patterns in the Tallahassee Hills. Unpublished manuscript.

Peebles, Christopher S. 1974. Moundville: The Organization of a Prehistoric Community and Culture. Ph.D. dissertation, University of California, Santa Barbara.

———. 1979. *Excavations at Moundville: 1905–1951.* Ann Arbor: University of Michigan Press.

———. 1981. Archaeological Research at Moundville: 1840–1980. *Southeastern Archaeological Conference Bulletin* 24:77–81.

———. ed. 1983. *Prehistoric Agricultural Communities of West Alabama,* 3 vols. Report to USACOE, Mobile, and USDOI-HCRS, Atlanta. Available from U.S. Army Corps of Engineers, Mobile District.

Peebles, Christopher S., and Susan M. Kus. 1977. Some Archaeological Correlates of Ranked Societies. *American Antiquity* 42:421–48.

Peebles, Christopher S., and Margaret J. Schoeninger. 1981. Notes on the Relationship between Social Status and Diet at Moundville. *Southeastern Archaeological Conference Bulletin* 24:96–97.

Peebles, Christopher S., Margaret J. Schoeninger, Vincas Steponaitis, and C. Margaret Scarry. 1981. A Precious Bequest: Contemporary Research with WPA-CCC Collections from Moundville. *Annals of the New York Academy of Sciences* 376:433–46.

Pelletier, Kenneth. 1977. *Mind as Healer, Mind as Slayer.* New York: Delacorte.

Perrin, N. 1974. *The New Testament: An Introduction.* New York: Harcourt Brace Jovanovich.

———. 1976. *Rediscovering the Teaching of Jesus.* New York: Harper & Row.

______. 1977. *The Resurrection According to Matthew, Mark and Luke*. Philadelphia: Fortress Press.

Perzigian, A. J., and L. Widmer. 1979. Evidence for Tuberculosis in a Prehistoric Population. *Journal of the American Medical Association* 241:2643–46.

Poswell, B. D. 1976. Coccidioidomycosis and North American Blastomycosis: Differential Diagnosis of Bone Lesions in Pre-Columbian American Indians. *American Journal of Physical Anthropology* 44:199.

Powell, Mary Lucas. 1981. Implications of Ranked Social Status for Physical Health and Development. Unpublished manuscript.

Price, James A., and James B. Griffin. 1979. *The Snodgrass Site of the Powers Phase of Southeast Missouri*. Anthropological Papers of the Museum of Anthropology, University of Michigan, No. 70. Ann Arbor: University of Michigan Press.

Quarantelli, E. L. 1954. The Nature and Conditions of Panic. *American Journal of Sociology* 60:267–75.

______. 1960. Images of Withdrawal Behavior in Disasters: Some Basic Misconceptions. *Social Problems* 8:68–79.

Rayón, Jose Garcia. 1965 [1581]. *Descripcion del Pueblo de Gueytlalpan (30 de Mayo 1581), Por El Alcaldo Mayor: Juan de Carrion*. Cuadernos de la Facultad de Filosofia, Letras, y Ciencias No. 23. Veracruz: Universidad Veracruzana.

Reck, Gregory G. 1978. *In the Shadow of Tlaloc: Life in a Mexican Village*. New York: Penguin Books.

Redfield, Robert. 1947. The Folk Society. *American Journal of Sociology* 42:293–308.

______. *1953. The Primitive World and Its Transformations*. Ithaca, N.Y.: Cornell University Press.

______. 1956. *Peasant Society and Culture: Anthropological Approach to Civilization*. Chicago: University of Chicago Press.

______. 1962. Civilization. In *Human Nature and the Study of Society: The Papers of Robert Redfield*, ed. Margaret Park Redfield, 364–414. Chicago: University of Chicago Press.

Reicke, B. 1964. *The Epistles of James, Peter and Jude: Introduction, Translation and Notes*. Anchor Bible, vol. 37. Garden City, N.Y.: Doubleday.

Renfrew, Colin. 1979a. *Before Civilization*. Cambridge: Cambridge University Press.

______. 1979b. *Investigation in Orkney*. London: Society of Antiquaries.

Rhein, F. B. 1966. *An Analytical Approach to the New Testament*. Woodbury, N.Y.: Barron's Educational Series.

Ribeiro, Darcy. 1968. *The Civilizational Process.* Washington, D.C.: Smithsonian Institution Press.

Richardson, Miles. 1975. Anthropologist—Myth Teller. *American Ethnologist* 2:517–33.

Ritchie, W. A. 1952. Pathological Evidence Suggesting Pre-Columbian Tuberculosis in New York State. *American Journal of Physical Anthropology* 10:305–17.

Robbins, Louise M. 1977. The Story of Life Revealed by the Dead. In *Biocultural Adaptation in Prehistoric America,* ed. R. L. Blakely, 10–26. Proceedings of the Southern Anthropological Society, No. 11. Athens: University of Georgia Press.

Rowland, Dunbar, and Alfred G. Sanders, eds. 1932. *Mississippi Provincial Archives 1704–1743 French Dominion.* Jackson: Mississippi Department of Archives and History.

Rowlands, Michael J. 1982. Processual Archaeology as a Historical Science. In *Theory and Explanation in Archaeology,* ed. Colin Renfrew, Michael J. Rowlands, and B. Abbot Segraves, 155–95. New York: Academic Press.

Rudolph, J. L. 1980. Beaverdam Creek Mound and Village: Interim Report. Manuscript on file, Department of Anthropology, University of Georgia.

Ruef, J. 1977. *Paul's First Letter to Corinth.* Philadelphia: Westminster Press.

Ruffer, M. A. 1921. Pott's Disease in an Egyptian Mummy from 21 Dynasty (1000 B.C.). In *Studies of Paleopathology in Egypt,* ed. R. L. Moodie. Chicago: University of Chicago Press.

Russell, D. S. 1968. *Between the Testaments.* Philadelphia: Fortress Press.

Salley, A. S. 1929. *Records in the British Public Records Office Relating to South Carolina 1685–1690.* Columbia: Historical Commission of South Carolina.

______. 1931. *Records in the British Public Records Office Relating to South Carolina 1691–1697.* Columbia: Historical Commission of South Carolina.

______. 1947. *Records in the British Public Records Office Relating to South Carolina 1701–1710.* Columbia: Historical Commission of South Carolina.

Sanders, William T., and Barbara J. Price. 1968. *Mesoamerica: The Evolution of Civilization.* New York: Random House.

Sandmel, S. 1958. *The Genius of Paul.* New York: Farrar, Straus & Cudahy.

______. 1960. *A Jewish Understanding of the New Testament.* New York: University Publishers.

Saul, Frank P. 1972. *The Human Skeletal Remains of Altar de Sacrificios: An Osteobiographic Analysis.* Papers of the Peabody Museum of Archaeology and Ethnology, No. 63. Cambridge, Mass.: Harvard University Press.

Savage, Henry, Jr. 1979. *Discovering America.* New York: Harper & Row.

Scarry, C. Margaret. 1981a. The University of Michigan Moundville Excavations: 1978–1979. *Southeastern Archaeological Conference Bulletin* 24:87–90.

———. 1981b. Plant Procurement Strategies in the West Jefferson and Moundville I Phases. *Southeastern Archaeological Conference Bulletin* 24:94–96.

Scarry, John. 1984. Fort Walton Development: Mississippian Chiefdoms in the Lower Southeast. Ph.D. dissertation, Case Western Reserve University, Cleveland, Ohio.

Scarry, John, and Claudine Payne. 1981. Mississippian Polities in the Fort Walton Area: Application and Evaluation of the Renfrew-Level XTENT Model. Unpublished manuscript.

Schanche, Don A. 1974. The Emotional Aftermath of "The Largest Tornado Ever." *Today's Health* 52:16–19, 61, 63–65.

Schillebeeckx, E. 1979. *Jesus: An Experiment in Christology.* New York: Seabury Press.

Schulberg, Herbert C. 1974. Disaster, Crisis Theory, and Intervention Strategies. *Omega* 5:77–87.

Schultz, Duane P. 1964. *Panic Behavior.* New York: Random House.

Schwartz, T. 1971. The Noise. *Psychology Today* 4(10):51–54, 102–3.

Schweizer, E. 1980. The Concept of the Davidic "Son of God" in Acts and Its Old Testament Background. In *Studies in Luke-Acts,* ed. L. E. Keck and J. L. Martyn, 186–93. Philadelphia: Fortress Press.

Scott, E. F. 1951. *The Literature of the New Testament.* New York: Columbia University Press.

Selby, D. J. 1962. *Toward the Understanding of St. Paul.* Englewood Cliffs, N.J.: Prentice-Hall.

Selye, Hans. 1956. *The Stress of Life.* New York: McGraw-Hill.

Shadomy, H. J. 1981. The Differential Diagnosis of Various Fungal Pathogens and Tuberculosis in the Prehistoric Indians. In *Prehistoric Tuberculosis in the Americas,* ed. J. E. Buikstra, 25–34. Evanston, Ill.: Northwestern University Archaeological Program.

Sheldon, Craig. 1974. The Mississippian-Historic Transition in Central Alabama. Ph.D. dissertation, University of Oregon, Eugene.

Sidel, Victor W. 1966. Medical Aspects of Civil Defense. In *Civil Defense,* ed. Henry Eyring, 53–75. Washington, D.C.: American Association for the Advancement of Science.

Siporin, Max. 1976. Altruism, Disaster, and Crisis Intervention. In *Emergency and Disaster Management,* ed. Howard J. Parad, H. L. P. Resnik, and Libbie G. Parad, 213–29. Bowie, Md.: Charles Press.

Smith, Bruce D., ed. 1978. *Mississippian Settlement Patterns.* New York: Academic Press.

Snell, William R. 1972. Indian Slavery in Colonial South Carolina, 1671–1795. Ph.D. dissertation, University of Alabama.

Staniforth, M. 1968. *Early Christian Writings: The Apostolic Fathers.* Baltimore, Md.: Penguin Books.

Steinbock, R. T. 1976. *Paleopathological Diagnosis and Interpretation.* Springfield, Ill.: Thomas.

Steponaitis, Vincas P. 1978. Location Theory and Complex Chiefdoms: A Mississippian Example. In *Mississippian Settlement Patterns,* ed. Bruce D. Smith, 417–54.

———. 1981a. Chronology and Community Patterns at Moundville. *Southeastern Archaeological Conference Bulletin* 24:99–104.

———. 1981b. Placquemine Ceramic Chronology in the Natchez Region. *Mississippi Archaeology* 16:6–19.

Stern, Gerald M. 1976. *The Buffalo Creek Disaster.* New York: Random House.

Stone, M. E. 1973. Judaism at the Time of Christ. *Scientific American* 228(1):80–87.

Strachey, James. 1962. Introduction. In Sigmund Freud, *Civilization and Its Discontents.* New York: Norton.

Swanton, John R. 1911. *Indian Tribes of the Lower Mississippi Valley and Adjacent Coast of the Gulf of Mexico.* Bureau of American Ethnology, Bulletin 43. Washington, D.C.: Government Printing Office.

———. 1922. *Early History of the Creek Indians and Their Neighbors.* Bureau of American Ethnology, Bulletin 73. Washington, D.C.: Government Printing Office.

———. 1946. *Indians of the Southeastern United States.* Bureau of American Ethnology, Bulletin 137. Washington, D.C.: Government Printing Office.

Sweet, Henry. 1855. *The Oldest English Texts.* London: Oxford University Press.

Sweet, J. P. M. 1979. *Revelation.* Philadelphia: Westminster Press.

Talmon, S. 1971. The New Covenanters of Qumran. *Scientific American* 225(5):72–81.

Terry, Clinton W. 1981. Police Stress: The Empirical Evidence. *Journal of Police Science and Administration* 9:61–75.

Theissen, G. 1978. *Sociology of Early Palestinian Christianity.* Philadelphia: Fortress Press.

Thomas, Cyrus H. 1894. Report on the Mound Exploration of the Bureau of Ethnology. In *Twelfth Annual Report of the Bureau of Ethnology,* 17–742. Washington, D.C.: Government Printing Office.

Thomas, William I., and Dorothy Swaine Thomas. 1938. *The Child in America.* New York: Knopf.

Throckmorton, B. H., Jr. 1967. *Gospel Parallels: A Synopsis of the First Three Gospels*. Nashville: Thomas Nelson.

Titchener, James L. 1970. Management and Study of Psychological Response to Trauma. *Journal of Trauma* 10:974–80.

Tödt, H. E. 1965. *The Son of Man in the Synoptic Tradition*. Philadelphia: Westminster Press.

Tuckman, Alan J. 1973. Disaster and Mental Health Intervention. *Community Mental Health Journal* 9:151–57.

Tylor, Edward B. 1920. *Primitive Culture*. New York: Putnam.

Unamuno, Miguel de. 1972. *The Tragic Sense of Life in Men and Nations*. Princeton, N.J.: Princeton University Press.

Valentine, C. 1963. Social Status, Political Power, and Native Responses to European Influence in Oceania. *Anthropological Forum* 1:3–35.

Van der Leeuw, Sander. 1981. Preliminary Report on the Analysis of Moundville Phase Ceramic Technology. *Southeastern Archaeological Conference Bulletin* 24:105–8.

Vielhauer, P. 1980. On the "Paulinism" of Arts. In *Studies in Luke-Acts*, ed. L. E. Keck and J. L. Martyn, 33–50. Philadelphia: Fortress Press.

Wagley, Charles. 1965. On the Concept of Social Race in the Americas. In *Contemporary Cultures and Societies of Latin America*, ed. D. B. Heath and R. N. Adams, 531–45. New York: Random House.

Wallace, Anthony F. C. 1956. *Tornado in Worcester*. Washington, D.C.: National Academy of Sciences, National Research Council.

Wallerstein, Immanuel. 1979. *The Capitalist World-Economy: Essays by Immanuel Wallerstein*. London: Cambridge University Press.

Waselkov, Gregory. 1978. Evolution of Deer Hunting in the Eastern Woodlands. *Mid-Continental Journal of Archaeology* 3:15–34.

Webb, G. B. 1936. *Tuberculosis*. New York: Paul B. Hoeber.

Webb, M. C. 1969. The Role of Environment and of Environmental Determinism in Modern Cultural Evolutionism. *Human Mosaic* 3:97–111.

______. 1973. Hebrews, Hellenes and Historia: An Essay on the Prehistory of Anthropology. Paper presented at the eighth Annual Meeting of the Southern Anthropological Society, Wrightsville Beach, N.C., March 1973.

______. 1976. How the Hebrews Invented the Idea of God: An (Admittedly Speculative) Anthropological Reconstruction. Paper presented at the eleventh Annual Meeting of the Southern Anthropological Society, Atlanta, Ga., April 1976.

Welch, Paul D. 1981. The West Jefferson Phase: Terminal Woodland Tribal Society in West-Central Alabama. *Southeastern Archaeological Conference Bulletin* 24:81–83.

Wessman, James W. 1981. *Anthropology and Marxism.* Cambridge, Mass.: Schenkman.
West Virginia Department of Mental Health. N.d. Plan for Training Mental Health Personnel for Early Service to Disaster Victims. West Virginia Department of Mental Health.
Wheeler, Mortimer. 1968. *The Indus Civilization,* 3rd ed. New York: Cambridge University Press.
White, Leslie A. 1949. *The Science of Culture: A Study of Man and Civilization.* New York: Straus & Giroux.
———. 1959. *The Evolution of Culture: The Development of Civilization to the Fall of Rome.* New York: McGraw-Hill.
———. 1975. *The Concept of Cultural Systems.* New York: Columbia University Press.
White, Leslie A., with Beth Dillingham. 1973. *The Concept of Culture.* Minneapolis, Minn.: Burgess.
White, L. T., Jr. 1958. Dynamo and Virgin Reconsidered. *American Scholar* 27:183–94.
———. 1968. *Machina ex Deo: Essays in the Dynamism of Western Culture.* Cambridge, Mass.: MIT Press.
White, Lynn, Jr. 1969. The Historic Roots of Our Ecologic Crisis. In *The Subversive Science,* ed. Paul Shepard and Daniel McKinley, 341–51. Boston: Houghton Mifflin.
Whiteley, D. E. H. 1969. *Thessalonians in the Revised Standard Version: With Introduction and Commentary.* London: Oxford University Press.
Willey, Gordon, and Jeremy Sabloff. 1980. *A History of American Archaeology.* San Francisco: Freeman.
Williams, C. S. C. 1964. *A Commentary on the Acts of the Apostles.* London: Adam and Charles Black.
Wilson, E. 1959. *The Scrolls from the Dead Sea.* New York: Meridian Books.
Wolf, Eric R. 1955. Types of Latin American Peasantry. *American Anthropologist* 57:452–71.
———. 1957. Closed Corporate Peasant Communities in Mesoamerica and Central Java. *Southwestern Journal of Anthropology* 13:1–18.
———. 1959. *Sons of the Shaking Earth.* Chicago: University of Chicago Press.
Wolfenstein, Martha. 1957. *Disaster: A Psychological Essay.* New York: Free Press.
Worsley, P. 1968. *The Trumpet Shall Sound: A Study of "Cargo" Cults in Melanesia.* New York: Schocken Books.
Wright, G. E., and R. H. Fuller. 1960. *The Book of the Acts of God: Contemporary Scholarship Interprets the Bible.* Garden City, N.Y.: Doubleday.

Wright, Henry T., III. 1977. Recent Research on the Origin of the State. *Annual Review of Anthropology* 6:379–97.

———. 1983. Prestate Political Formations. Unpublished manuscript.

Wright, Henry T., III, and Gregory A. Johnson. 1975. Population, Exchange, and Early State Formation in Southwestern Iran. *American Anthropologist* 77:267–89.

Wright, J. Leitch, Jr. 1981. *The Only Land They Knew.* New York: Free Press.

Wright, J. V., and J. E. Anderson. 1969. *The Bennett Site.* Bulletin 229. Toronto: National Museum of Canada.

Young, J. Z. 1971. *An Introduction to the Study of Man.* New York: Oxford University Press.

Contributors

HANS A. BAER is an associate professor of anthropology at the University of Arkansas at Little Rock. His research interests include religion, medical pluralism, the political economy of health, and ethnicity. He has published articles on the Hutterites, Mormonism, black spiritual churches, black ethnomedicine, and osteopathy and chiropractic in the United States and Great Britain. He is the author of *The Black Spiritual Movement: A Religious Response to Racism* (University of Tennessee Press, 1984).

ROBERT L. BLAKELY is an associate professor of anthropology at Georgia State University in Atlanta. He received his B.A. and Ph.D. degrees in anthropology from Indiana University. With grants from the National Science Foundation, Blakely has conducted research on skeletons from the Etowah site, Oakland Cemetery in Atlanta, and the King site in Georgia. He edited *Biocultural Adaptation in Prehistoric America* (University of Georgia Press, 1977) and recently published "American Bioanthropology: A Personal Epistemology" (*Communication and Cognition,* 1984). Interests include paleodemography, paleoepidemiology, paleonutrition, and forensic anthropology. Blakely has served as proceedings editor for the Southern Anthropological Society and as president of the society.

MARSHALL DURBIN, an associate professor of anthropology at Washington University, died suddenly of asthma on December 16, 1983. An anthropological linguist, he specialized in theory and in the study of American Indian languages. He was also dedicated to training native Americans to do linguistic analysis, and regarded his informants as consultants and co-researchers. At the time of his death, he was scheduled to go to Brazil as a Fulbright Scholar.

EDWARD L. GREENAMYRE is an associate professor of anthropology at Tennessee Technological University and a consultant to the Tennessee Emergency Management Agency. His ongoing research interests, which were initially based upon field investigations conducted in Japan, concern the medical and legal implications of environmental problems. His published writings cover such subjects as crisis intervention, the triage concept in emergency medical services, protection of elderly and handicapped citizens in civil disaster situations, nuclear emergency communications procedures, and the functional limits of formalism in anthropological research. In 1983 he was decorated by the federal government for original technical research considered instrumental in raising the quality of health care available to victims of catastrophic situations and collective stress.

JOSEPH V. GUILLOTTE III is an associate professor of anthropology at the University of New Orleans. He received his Ph.D. from Tulane University. He has studied social and cultural integration in a multiethnic community in Tanzania, has been involved in nutritional research in Zaire, and has most recently done fieldwork among fishermen and trappers in southern Louisiana.

ARDEN R. KING is a professor emeritus in anthropology at Tulane University, New Orleans. His extensive career has included fieldwork among North American Indians and American blacks, and he has also worked in Guatemala and North Germany.

DAVID S. MATHEWS holds B.A. and M.A. degrees in anthropology from Georgia State University in Atlanta. His M.A. thesis, "The Battle of Mabila: The Ulibahali Casualties from the King Site," is the first work to link archaeologically recovered Native American casualties to a sixteenth-century Spanish expedition in the interior southeastern United States. Mathews's interests include skeletal biology, forensic anthropology, southeastern archaeology, and computer analyses. He is currently employed as an electronic design engineer for a computer software firm in Atlanta.

CHRISTOPHER S. PEEBLES has been a member of the Albert Egges van Giffin Institute for Pre- and Protohistory, University of Amsterdam, and the Research Center for Language and Semiotic Studies, Indiana University. He is currently director of the Glenn A. Black Laboratory of Archaeology, Indiana University. He has been a visiting associate professor of anthropology at Pennsylvania State University and an adjunct associate professor of anthropology at the University of Alabama. The major focus of his research has been the prehistory of the southeastern United States, particularly the Moundville, Alabama, area. He also maintains an active interest in the protohistoric period and archaeology of northern Europe, especially the interaction of Germanic and Celtic groups with the outposts of the Roman Empire. In addition, Peebles constructs large-scale computer databases and management information systems for archaeological research projects, and "knowledge-based" systems for historic preservation programs.

GREGORY G. RECK is a professor of anthropology at Appalachian State University in Boone, North Carolina. He has carried out field research in east-central Mexico and in southern Appalachia and is the author of *In the Shadow of Tlaloc: Life in a Mexican Village* (Penguin Books, 1978). He is currently engaged in research projects on ethnicity, class, and education in southern Appalachia and on the nature and significance of narrative forms in anthropological writing.

MILES RICHARDSON, a member of the Southern Anthropological Society since its organizational meeting in 1965, has served the society as secretary-treasurer, president, chair of the James Mooney Award Committee, and (twice) program chair. His anthropological interests center on the ways in which people use artifacts to construct their worlds. He also writes fiction and has recently published a story, "The Museum," about who owns the past: the Indians who made it, or the archaeologists who dig it up? Another story about an anthropologist won second prize in the Deep South Writer's Conference of 1984.

MALCOLM C. WEBB is a professor of anthropology and coordinator for anthropology in the Department of Anthropology and Geography at the University of New Orleans. He received his Ph.D. from the University of Michigan in 1964. His regional specialties are the prehistory of Mesoamerica and the Gulf Coast of the United States. His topical interests include economic anthropology and the anthropology of religion, with special attention to the role of trade in chiefdoms and early states, the role of religion as a vehicle of economic and social integration, and the rise of state societies. He has served as president of the Southern Anthropological Society and as editor of its newsletter, the *Southern Anthropologist*.

Index